Charles de Gaulle

Charles de Gaulle

Futurist of the Nation

———◆———

RÉGIS DEBRAY

Translated by John Howe

VERSO
London · New York

First published by Verso 1994
© Verso 1994
All rights reserved

Verso
UK: 6 Meard Street, London W1V 3HR
USA: 29 West 35th Street, New York, NY 10001-2291

Verso is the imprint of New Left Books

ISBN 0 86091 622 7
ISBN 0 86091 452 6 (pbk)

British Library Cataloguing in Publication Data
A catalogue record for this book is available from the British Library

Library of Congress Cataloging-in-Publication Data
Debray, Régis.
[A demain de Gaulle. English]
Charles de Gaulle, futurist of the nation / Régis Debray ;
translated by John Howe.
p.   cm.
Translation of: A demain de Gaulle.
ISBN 0-86091-622-7—ISBN 0-86091-452-6 (pbk.)
1. Gaulle, Charles de, 1890–1970—Political and social views.
2. Presidents—France—Biography. 3. France—Politics and
government—20th century. 4. France—Foreign relations—20th
century. I. Title.
DC420.D41813   1994
944.083'6'092—dc20
[B]

Typeset by Solidus (Bristol) Limited
Printed and bound in Great Britain by
Biddles Ltd, Guildford and King's Lynn

This book has been published with the financial assistance of
the French Ministry of Culture.

Contents

Foreword to the

English edition

The great French novelist Albert Cohen managed to export
Churchill across the Channel. Cohen, who reached London in
1940, achieved his miracle in the middle of the Blitz with the lyrical
poem *Churchill d'Angleterre* which, half a century later, can still make
us see and feel the soul of Great Britain. Times have changed,
though, and I cannot lay claim to a comparable literary talent: I
cannot hope to get Charles of France intact across the Channel. The
cliché-covered gravestone is too heavy. And how does one preserve
some freedom of thought between the pomposities of official
courtesy on the one hand and, on the other, the unshakeable
suspicion with which many of my British friends regard an archaic,
ungrateful xenophobe, authoritarian and vaguely fascist? Neither
the worldwide dissemination of images and capital, nor the digging
of the Channel Tunnel, alters the fact that caricatures travel better
than portraits. After all, the bowlers, umbrellas and thin drizzle of
the City do not travel either, any more than the morning *sfumato* in
the hills of Siena or the bouquet of a great Bordeaux. I am afraid
that, like them, this victorious soldier, who disdained the military
and placed the writer above the warrior, may have to be consumed in
his country of origin. All we know about foreign cultures – and those
closest to us are in a way the most inaccessible – is their surface glitter
and misleading details. De Gaulle – vast deep-sea creature, super-
lucid coelacanth – cruises the murky depths unseen.

People on the Left – let us admit it – have good reasons not to
penetrate below the surface of things, and where de Gaulle is
concerned this is particularly true of the British, whatever their

political colour. Our Jesuit-educated Papist carried Ireland in his heart, the Ireland of the Stuarts and of O'Connell. Between Perfidious Albion and this remote descendant of the McCartans, in fact, there always loomed memories of Crécy, Agincourt, Waterloo and Fashoda. I imagine that obstacles of this sort work in both directions, and the veto on British entry to the Common Market can hardly have improved matters.

De Gaulle, who had a deep and long-standing knowledge of Germany, visited the United Kingdom for the first time on 9 June 1940. He spoke German well, but to the end of his days he affected a mumbled and incoherent English. Suddenly, on 16 June 1940, this traditional Anglophobe embraced the astonishing project for a 'Franco–British Union' (two countries, one nation), and then gradually formed with Churchill a set of 'fabulous twins' (Jean Lacouture) locked, like all couples, in a love–hate relationship with countless tragicomic side-effects. I do not know whether de Gaulle ever loved Britain; he used to say that states have allies, not friends. I do not know whether the Britain of today still has anything in common with the Britain of 1940. I am sure of only one thing: that if any readers of my generation have a familiar, attractive and romantic image of Britain, they owe it not to André Maurois, nor even to Voltaire's *Lettres anglaises*, but to de Gaulle's *Mémoires*. I do not believe that any other Frenchman since the Battle of Hastings has made the hereditary enemy so likeable to his fellow countrymen as this champion of the national interest, who unhesitatingly made London the capital of France for four years.

In 1990, as the centenary of the General's birth approached, Bernard Tricot (director of the Institut Charles de Gaulle) asked several personalities on the Left, including myself, how they felt about de Gaulle. As the memories trickled back, the resulting article – almost without my knowing it – turned into a book. So *A demain de Gaulle* was the product of chance, at a moment when I was becoming a philosopher and writer once again, having recently resigned from the post of adviser to François Mitterrand and given up politics. We all know the clichés about this sort of thing: what could be more commonplace than someone who was a Leftist at twenty doing a U-turn at forty, cashing in his youthful amours with a fine new career in the establishment? Sorry, but the hat does not fit. I have not become a nationalist or a conservative. It was as an utterly incorrigible left-wing socialist that I undertook this study of a rebel, a lonely man, but also – and above all – one whose wisdom was genuinely philosophic.

All de Gaulle's predictions – the transience of world communism, the reunification of Germany, the resurrection of the old Russia, the collapse of the empires, and so on – have come true since his death. There is no Gaullian doctrine, but nobody who thinks about history can avoid trying to understand this extraordinary insight into things, except perhaps by seeing it as supernatural, like the insight of a fakir or a medium. Its essence lies in balancing the permanent against the accidental, the long term against the short vision. This man, whose thought was remarkably free in terms of the opinions and formulae of his period, his class and even his country, never fell for the economistic illusion common to yesterday's Marxists and the liberals of today. He put his trust in the depth of time, in that sort of collective genetic code known as the spirit of a people, which over time sets into the living individuality called a 'nation'. A terrible word, an ambiguous word; a word of which you can make what you want. An ethnic nation, backward and medieval, founded on the law of blood, earth and the dead; or an elective nation, founded on the law of the soil and voluntary participation in a common project. Pétain or de Gaulle, Teutonic forest or French Revolution. Now that the Europe of Brussels is making it clear to everyone that the economic and financial stuff alone will not make a Community, it could be that the old dilemma, federalism versus nationalism, is giving place to a new one: de Gaulle's nation versus Le Pen's tribe. That is why it is relevant to look back down the road at a statesman who was visionary only to the extent that he was archaic. Retrograde progress is the paradox of our age: the more modern the machines, the more archaic the mentalities. The crucial thing is to know whether we are going to plunge back into the forest, or manage to live in a good understanding with others by staying faithful to what we are.

'Everyone is, has been or will be Gaullist,' runs the well-known saying. Personally, although I had always savoured de Gaulle's foreign policy in a more or less furtive manner, I did not admit my intellectual 'Gaullism' to myself until 1968, in Bolivia, in prison.

The moment might almost have been chosen for the irony of its contradictions. Anyway, the Latin Quarter was not ready for that sort of medicine. But Che's defeat made me understand that the World Revolution is not a mother country, that in the long run national connections count for more than class or ideological commitments. It was as a 'left-wing Gaullist' that President Mitterrand recruited me into his Cabinet; and it was as such that I left it. In the interim I tried, in two or three books (*La Puissance et les rêves, Les Empires contre l'Europe*), to sketch an outline of what a Left realpolitik, equidistant from conservative cynicism and 'progressive' Pollyannaism, might be, or might have been. Some have seen this small examination of conscience as representing a more or less scandalous break with my past and my socialist friends (despite the fact that I have never joined the party of that name). I hope I have made it clear that it is neither a renunciation nor a change of direction: just a farewell signing-off after ten years of vain effort, in the context of responsible political practice, to reconcile the strength of a conviction with the force of circumstances.

RÉGIS DEBRAY
Paris, 1993

1

Don't think I'm boasting

Please don't give me any of that stuff about youth being the future of the world.

I was twenty. I remember marching under banners that said 'No to fascism!' We had our doubts. 'Really?' we asked our elders. 'Fascism? The real thing?'

'Don't be pedantic, lads. Look at it this way: ever heard of Bonapartism?' Well yes, OK, that was in our history books: *coup d'état* and plebiscite. So it was going to be the Third Empire. If it worked. Or the Praetorians if it didn't.

I remember posters showing a tall paunchy silhouette topped with a képi, getting ready to gag Marianne from behind. I remember the leaflets: 'Halt personal power!' 'Franco, Salazar, de Gaulle.' I remember the Mitterrand of those days, dogged and pessimistic: 'After the generals come the colonels. After Neguib, Nasser.' I remember Maurice Thorez and his 'calls to struggle'. 'Bread, liberty and peace for all the French.' For starvation, dictatorship and war lurked just round the corner. I remember 'relative pauperization' and 'State monopoly capitalism'.

And never mind the actual individual; that was just eyewash. I remember that we never talked about de Gaulle but about 'Gaullist power': the power of banks, trusts and monopolies, our unknown enemies.

I remember the rhythmic blare of car horns in the Champs-Élysées: *Al-gér-ie française*. I remember 'Je vous ai compris', insurgents on the barricades, the fascist *pieds-noirs* Ortiz and

Lagaillarde, the 'quarter-pound* of retired generals'. I remember not having found a car on the night when the Prime Minister, Michel Debré, urged the people of Paris to stop the paras by going 'on foot or by car' to surround the military airfields.

I remember Eddie Constantine and his sailor's hat, the unhappy Queen Soraya, Miles Davis's muted trumpet in *Lift to the Scaffold*. I remember Albert Camus meeting his end in a mangled Facel Vega, Audrey Hepburn's ponytail, the extraordinary hit made by *Zazie dans le métro*. I remember the Ballets roses, France's one-man equivalent of the Profumo scandal, and the first Paris–Tokyo flight over the North Pole.

I remember a good book, *Le Style du général*, in which Jean-François Revel, with great precision, dissected the Grand Panjandrum's affected archaisms, errors of syntax and false flourishes, concluding (for the style is the man) that de Gaulle was wholly lacking in 'a statesman's nature'.

I remember Georges Perec just back from Tunisia, his wild hair cut short, the little wart on his nose. 'L'œil, d'abord, glisserait sur la moquette grise ...' This was to be called: 'a story of the 1960s'. *Things* was already breaking through behind *La Ligne générale*, the critical Marxist periodical he edited. We used to meet at his place in the evenings, watched by the benevolent shades of Henri Lefebvre and Bertolt Brecht ... the projected revue never saw the light of day. Neither did the Line, fortunately for him. They would have cost him a lot of time.

I remember the class of 1960 at Louis-le-Grand. The Communists set the tone, and only a handful of timorous souls admitted to being 'Mendésists'. I remember a rumour one day that had us bursting with pride. The *cacique* of a previous class, representing the student body during some ceremony at the École normale, had refused to shake hands with the General-President, who (another provocation by big capital!) had had the temerity to attend in person. Officials open-mouthed with dismay, senior staff apoplectic; to me it was sublime, like the barricades of 2 December

---

*(*Trans.*) *Quarteron*. See footnote below, p. 23.

... 'You shall see how a man can die for twenty-five francs.' Whether the rumour was true or false, I remember attacking my Latin and Greek with redoubled zeal in order to become *cacique* in my turn. I dreamed of repeating this feat of arms the next time a representative of the bourgeoisie ventured into our fortress. The first aim achieved, I awaited my chance for the second, but in vain. Nobody showed up. The enemy cut us dead.

Those were the thanks de Gaulle received for his visit, the last made to the rue d'Ulm by a President of the French Republic. Neither Pompidou (because of '68, and although he was a *normalien* himself), nor Giscard (because d'Estaing), nor Mitterrand (because of the adman Seguela), has since deigned to honour with his presence our temple of jeering, up-to-the-minute little swots. But how were we to know? Meanwhile, we were not encumbered with an excess of delicacy.

*

The infuriating old lummox was digging in for a long stay, so it was I who had to leave. The World Revolution was calling, but in my case there was another factor, a sort of exasperation connected with my surname. Prime Minister, first of the Companions, first in everything, Michel Debré spelt his name differently from my own, but it sounded exactly the same. I spent the best part of my adolescence spelling out the *a-y* of my own name loudly and clearly through gritted teeth, across counters, down the telephone, in classrooms. The whole thing was gratuitous, as I would have been anti-Gaullist in any case. By 1961 I had had enough. The Debré loophole covered the whole Hexagon,* and I was not going to get my *a-y* recognized at home (especially in the shadow of that ghastly General-President). There are people who go abroad to make a name for themselves. Was it to recuperate mine that I left for Latin America?

I have to ask for forgiveness.

For being so boringly self-obsessed. I agree that relating all these

---

*(*Trans.*) France, whose shape on the map is roughly hexagonal.

trivia to such a monolithic sculpted figure, one whose staying power finally made him virtually an abstraction, verges on the indecent. But I am not doing it out of narcissism and self-satisfaction. I do it because of the need for openness. This agonizing investigation was started by Bernard Tricot's question, posed – innocently or otherwise – to contemporaries of all sorts: 'Where do you stand in relation to de Gaulle?'. It forced me to acknowledge that for many years, where the late General is concerned, I have had the uneasy feeling of being in arrears – like an insensitive debtor who no longer bothers to cross the road to avoid his creditor. Because the fact is that I owe him a great deal.

My life, for a start, by virtue of a telegram sent from Paris to General Barrientos a few days after my arrest. You may think that is not much, and you may be right. But I owe him far more than that. I owe him the intelligence, such as it is, that I have been able to gather from the time I live in. And I gave him nothing in return. It is with a defaulter's sheepish air that I now render belated homage, and I will never forgive myself for this failure. By the time I came out of prison he was in the cemetery. I never even managed a thank-you letter. All right, I am talking big, OK. I would never have dared write to de Gaulle, let alone talk to him face to face. I would have gulped a stiffener in every bar between Paris and Colombey, arrived legless at La Boisserie, collapsed mute and slobbering on the doorstep: who *is* this tiresome bore? I am not the king's cousin, you know. In my dreams I am on terms of easy familiarity with Louis XI, with Lenin, Edison and Lincoln. But I quail before de Gaulle. He is the Great Other, the inaccessible absolute. Even during the hours of darkness.

That is why his name carries a flavour of remorse, of delay too great to be made up, of debt which can never be repaid. Say de Gaulle, my friends, and we will try to hold back our tears. I envy the louts who, at the mention of that name, stick their chests out and wave the flag. All I can do is look down at my toes. There have been too many misdeals. To find the rebel, I turned my back on him; to reach 1940 London, I fled from 1960 Paris. How often are commitments the product, not even of idealism, but of *affectation*? Same arrangement, different components: guerrilla warfare in the role of the maquis, Yankees instead of Nazis, Guevara as the de

Gaulle of the Andes, Fidel as a younger, cigar-chomping Churchill. London calling, Havana calling, La Paz calling. Free men calling free men.

Poetry and action are not very domestic. The shattering nature of early Latin American novels, and encumbrances at home, made emigration seem advisable. How could one imagine in those days that Europe, facing the two empires, would turn out to have a playable hand? Or that it was possible to wage one's little war at home, without swagger, but ultimately on a more serious basis? The second-stage romanticism, the prosaic clarity of vision needed to make the attempt, would have demanded a level of renunciation, of self-abnegation, that was wholly beyond me at the time. I do not regret my mistakes, but it took me quite a while to open my eyes.

I became a 'Gaullist' – the term is incorrect but appropriate – around May 1968. A bit late, you might think, but better late than never. Remember the poor idiots of the time who imagined that the CRS were just like the SS. It was the Guarani Indians of the Chaco who recruited me, affiliated me to that discredited brotherhood; convinced me that what is immaterial about a nation, a culture or a memory may constitute the ultimate axis for historical action. The Indians of the Bolivian Chaco did not speak Marxist, but this (although regrettable) was not unexpected: the same had been true of the Chinese peasants in Yunnan thirty years earlier. The problem with this lot was that they did not even speak Spanish. Che made speeches, gave them the word; they understood not a word, not a single blessed syllable. Between them and us there was only a missing language, practically nothing, and that was all. An impenetrable wall of adobe and distrust. Curtains. Death. This experience, and one or two others, gradually taught me that the World Revolution is not a mother country, not even a field of activity, but, at best, a subject for speculation. That 'professional revolutionaries' – the feudal elite of internationalism to which I thought for a time that I belonged – just skate over the surface of events, wandering zombies noxious to their own cause, without leverage on the grain of things. In a word, that it is always right to revolt, but it is a good idea to know for what and against whom. Being knocked about in prison makes the best of universities for university men. It ought to be compulsory.

Don't think I'm boasting. I just had the good fortune at that time not to be among my own, my brothers in delirium, those generous idealists who lacked only distance and perspective. I know that people often end up achieving the opposite of what they intend, that the cock-up principle reigns supreme over our lives, but I will never overcome my astonishment at what occurred: the Don Quixotes of the Latin Quarter taking on the country's last Don Quixote and giving a leg-up to Sancho Panza. Taking a prophet for a notary, and vice versa. Going straight from an *An* II (Mark 2) to a Second Empire (Mark 2). Straight from Free Radio to Radio Dosh; from social experiment to private enterprise; from workers' council to board of management. We may not have ruined our lives, but we missed the boat all right.

*

We were not without excuses for our wanderings. Is this plural employed for dubious reasons of modesty? Well then: I was on the wrong continent, following the wrong great man in the wrong epic. In the proud singular, I enter a plea of extenuating circumstances.

It was the early 1960s, and the time was nigh. People railed against the obsolete type of man whose failings were going to prevent France from answering the call. It was predicted on all sides that the new man was coming. But where from? People argued about this cardinal point, although the imminence of the apocalypse was not in doubt. Partisans of the West projected a millenarianism of the computer, management and the American challenge: salvation through Europe and technology. Partisans of the East projected an earlier millenarianism based on communisms, agropolises and Sputnik: salvation through soviets and electricity. Lastly, and a thousand times more seductively, came the partisans of the South with their black and beautiful anger: salvation through carnage and armed peasantries. Servan-Schreiber, Gagarin and Frantz Fanon did not agree on anything, except that de Gaulle was a dusty fetish and a regenerated humanity awaited us on the corner of the next decade. The first assured us that it would be globally aware, the second that it would be Communist, the third that it would be Third-Worldist; but whatever the details, one thing was certain: the time of nations and religions would soon be behind us. Servan-Schreiber noted the absence of flags in the offices of IBM; Gagarin had not met God in space; and Sartre diagnosed that Europe had had it. 'The European', he wrote in his preface to Fanon's seminal *Wretched of the Earth,* 'has managed to become a man only by manufacturing slaves and monsters.' That fat, pallid, self-obsessed continent had stopped being a subject of history and become a club of humanist executioners (Sétif, Hanoi, Madagascar, Algeria).... 'Let's drop this Europe, forever talking about humanity while massacring every human being it meets.' Anyway, that is what I did, and I am still not sorry.

Don't misunderstand me. I am not saying that I would rather have been wrong with Sartre than right with de Gaulle. Indeed, I am sorry that Sartre should have so misunderstood the reasoning of that pure European, de Gaulle. Even today it would cost me too much to have to choose between them. They were both authentic men, men who lived as they thought, without concealed contradictions.

I am not sure how much it bothered de Gaulle, but it is certainly a misfortune that with few exceptions, leading thinkers failed to take seriously the last of our philosopher-kings who took thought seriously. The intelligentsia ground its teeth in 1958 and screamed the place down in 1968, doubtless for good reasons. But the rest of the time, in all honesty, de Gaulle just made us snigger.

The course of events seems to be sorting out the wheat from the chaff, choosing between 'Marxism is the untranscendable horizon of our time' and 'The twenty-first century will either be spiritual or will not take place'. But Sartre was our oracle and Malraux just a clown. Which of the two was called in to enlighten the Sorbonne students in May '68?

I have lost the taste for self-flagellation, but I retain the custom of honouring losers. For twenty years de Gaulle and Malraux were ignored, repressed by the climate of the time. They are having their revenge now, but to what purpose? It is too late for me to pay my debts. And trumpet-blowing is tiring. I would just like to understand the real reasons for all our missed rendezvous. Why so many of us have turned up late in our own lives.

2

Leave your prejudices

outside

A successful incarnation, an *ism* round your neck, is a millstone that drags you straight to the bottom. A hundred years later, some float back to the surface, others do not. Marx, still shackled to his suffix, lies at fifteen hundred fathoms. No doubt he will soon reappear. Never mind the question of whether de Gaulle was a Gaullist in the same way that Marx was a Marxist (in other words, not at all). Gaullism has foundered and de Gaulle is emerging, restored to himself at last. Boulangism has disappeared too, but General Boulanger is still mouldering on the bottom. Bonapartism may be extinct, but we are still struck by something Napoleon did as soon as he reached Moscow: he issued the decree establishing the Comédie-Française.

Only death relieves the great man of the lackeys, detractors and courtiers who, in his lifetime, make him seem smaller by constantly shoving him in our faces. In the heat of the moment our own leanings make us confuse small idiocies with big ones, as an observer who is too committed confuses true immortals with false. But Time, Marguerite Yourcenar's 'great sculptor', plays no tricks. He awaits the end of the play before making the fake hero vanish in a puff of smoke: commonplace disillusion. It also happens, more rarely, that time reveals the crystalline hardness of what we once thought to be smoke.

De Gaulle would be a hundred this year (1990). In the twenty years since his death his outline has taken on substance rather than scale, as if the myth were posthumously regaining its flesh. God, what damage politics does to history!

*

A republican in 1869 would not have been able to get a very precise idea of Napoleon I's role by scrutinizing the rabble of 2 December encamped in the Tuileries. When he was writing *Napoléon le petit* in Guernsey, Victor Hugo took good care not to look so low. Looking at Marx through Stalin, Robespierre through Marchais or de Gaulle through the Gaullists of the day, just because the latter lay claim to the former, shows an aptitude for good relations and low polemic. In the twelfth century the Church established and legalized torture in the West. So what was there in Christ's message that permitted torture? The historian Péguy favoured 'comparing mystiques with mystiques and policies with policies'. Anyone can refute Gaullist policy in the name of socialist mystique. The opposite can also be done. Those who are tempted to do this forget that in the mangrove swamps of power, crocodiles devour cherubs of Left and Right with equal voracity. By what means can the vile be prevented from pouncing on the living? Or swindlers and cutthroats kept from infesting the coat-tails of yesterday's 'dear Companions', as they infest those of today's 'old friends'? It will be argued that the Gaullian knighthood *also* included men who were capable of dying for the founder of the Order of the Liberation. True, history has not confronted the first Mitterrandist circles with tests of the same sort, but this does not prove anything. Hitler and Ceauşescu, in their time, inspired impressive devotion in their followers. The exceptional fervour of Gaullists from the great days is not a sign of superiority in itself, any more than Christian martyrdoms prove the existence of God.

Personally I prefer the Left, the real Left. But I am willing to admit that, lullaby for lullaby, 'the old refrains of national incantation' are worth just as much as the timeworn chant of Peace-Justice-Progress-Liberty. Grant for a moment that the scep-tics are right, and that it is impossible to decide between these two *mystiques*. As to the *politics* that claim connection with them, neither is in a position, *a priori*, to teach the other anything. An English-man once described patriotism as 'the last refuge of a scoundrel'. Of what *ism* can this not be said? Yes, patriotism can be a business. So can socialism. To govern is to set up shop, which also means manning the storerooms and back-premises. When François Mitterrand, in opposition, called on people to reject 'the regime of personal power' and 're-create the citizens' Republic', he made a distinction between 'Gaullists of legend and Gaullists from the junk shop'. He meant that behind the screen provided by the former, the latter were feathering their nests. Twenty years on, it would be easy to return the compliment, so true is it that the Left of legend could not break the custom of lasting only a few weeks in office without paying the bill. Reasons of state always have a gamey side, and wheeling and dealing are inevitable. Even so, Lamartine's 'escendants have been more damaged by embezzlements and Greenpeace than Richelieu's ever were by secret police thugs and the construction business. In the end the big commercial bourgeoisie 'dropped' de Gaulle, who never made electoral capital by attacking big business; now it lives harmoniously with Mitterrand, whose mandate was to oppose it. And I must say I would like the man elected by the poor to arouse as much rancour in the financial press and the Stock Exchange as the 'representative of the big monopolies' did after 1968. Mitterrand is no more interested in money than de Gaulle was; his distaste for all that is perfectly genuine. But under his reign, money has run amok and swallowed the last islets of art, charity and sport. Under his reign, public television has been yielded up tamely to the advertising men.

At what point does an elected oligarchy make use of a Jaurès or a Joan of Arc in order to continue enjoying power, complete with limousines, outriders and official executive jet? The decisive moment of inflection is unconscious, blurred, impossible to assign to a specific date. I do not see that it has ever been avoided anywhere in the world, whatever the mystique, Christ, Lenin and Gandhi included. It is just a matter of time. The distance between Jean Moulin's Gaullism and the Gaullism of the 'thieves' kitchens' is the same as the distance between the socialism of Épinay and that of the boardroom: twenty years. 'Every man over thirty is a blackguard,' Borges says somewhere. We can say in the same spirit that every administration becomes an abuse of trust after ten years. Individual ethics have no more to do with it than the rival *isms*. It is a question of entropy. Right or Left, to endure is to fall.

11

Hardly more relevant here is the unchanging psychology of power-seekers. Does it include double-dealing, ingratitude, manipulation, bullying, secretiveness, arrogance, ambition, duplicity? Credible witnesses assure us that it does. Such, in fact, are the qualities of the sovereign, or the defects of all sovereignty: a functional cynicism has always been the minimum qualification for the profession. But these traits alone do not make a statesman. Intimates of the great Charles, who loathed familiarity, have given us glimpses of other aspects – the little-known humour, the shy kindnesses, the ardours of the man of feeling. Churchill noted that he concealed 'behind his impassive and impenetrable attitude a surprising sensitivity to pain'. The classic split between the public and the private. Mitterrand, who once criticized the General's public comportment as 'disagreeable to a democrat', has given offence countless times in the same way since becoming President himself. The simple fact is that power is disagreeable. Sensitive souls cannot cope, and moralists should stay well clear.

'Evangelic perfection does not lead to Empire' (de Gaulle, *Le Fil de l'épée*).

3

One myth per century?

Let us start by setting the facts aside and concentrating on serious matters – legends, for example.

Napoleon was the great political myth of the nineteenth century; de Gaulle of the twentieth.

The sublime, it seems, appears in France only once a century. Just as well for most of us, because it is an intrusion that decimates or exhausts us. Or at least messes us about. Napoleon left two generations dead on the battlefield. De Gaulle was more sparing with other people's blood; even so, he left us, as it were, stranded, alive but dazed.

What is a myth? A force that leaves a wake behind it. Where does the force come from? A shared dream. A delusion, perhaps, but one that turns the world upside down: causes events and movements; divides people into supporters and adversaries; leaves traces in the form of civil and penal codes and railways, factories and institutions (the Fifth Republic has already lasted three times as long as the Empire). A statesman who gets something going, who has followers, escapes the reality of reports and statistics to become part of the imagination. Napoleon and de Gaulle modified the state of things because they modified souls. They count as much for the solidity of what they built as for the intensity of the passions – both for and against – that they aroused. Hagiography, caricature, pamphlets, popular images. Dreams, fantasies, stereotypes, symbols. Both were mental and sentimental phenomena, and decisive for that reason. It's scandalous how immaterial and irrational they are, the forces that drive us . . .

At this point, political science stirs uneasily and leans forward in its chair. What odious, fallacious rhetoric! How can the exterminator be compared with the liberator? The great captain who had his political adversaries murdered with the great politician in general's uniform who benevolently granted them the right to reply, and never won a military victory in his life? The fact is that the former ran the whole enterprise into the ground, while the latter managed to save it. So that to measure the rebel against the despot, the challenger against the leader, is just glaringly idiotic. You simply do not put an adventurer who worked for himself or his family on the same level as a commander-in-chief serving his country. A 'corner-boy' from Ajaccio next to a 'great gentleman' born in Lille. Without considering the constantly changing format of a country in relation to the outside world, which gives its celebrities their variable standing on the world stage. Abbeville is not Austerlitz, Colombey is not St Helena. Nor was the gutless Hexagon of 1940 the great nation of 1810. Our heroes have dwindled with the Hexagon down the centuries.

Then again, what a poisoned chalice this analogy is! It puts the de Gaulle link in its proper place in the long chain of authoritarian populism that has been, and still is, the running sore of French democracy. Got him! Serge July will tell you triumphantly. Debray has unmasked himself! Scratch the republican and find the Bonapartist ... the repressed Caesarism of Jacobins in an authoritarian democracy, people who, at heart, really care only for its authoritarian side....

All the same, I am going to persist and put my name down. I have nothing more to lose, imagewise. I refrain from fooling about with dates: Waterloo fell on 18 June and the 18 Brumaire on 9 November ... the day the Emperor exits from history, the General enters; the day Napoleon arrives, Charles leaves.... No, none of that. Regrettably, Gaullism and Bonapartism have a number of features in common, but Napoleon and de Gaulle do not have the same moral value. The former is abominable to any republican, whereas the latter is acceptable. Nor do they have the same political meaning: Empire versus Kingdom, Europe through steel and Europe through co-operation, two opposing lineages. Napoleon is in the line of Charlemagne, de Gaulle in the line of Hugues

14

Capet. The first wanted a Holy French Empire without the faith, a Europe under French occupation. The second wanted to rescue the nation from the emperors and establish a free France in a free Europe. Wars are waged over smaller differences. Napoleon and de Gaulle were not on the same side; cousins, perhaps, but adversaries. The General detested the Emperor, with reason, but the two men ploughed the same furrow. 'Everyone has loved and hated me. Each has joined me, left me or rejoined me. There is not a Frenchman whom I have not moved' (Napoleon, at Las Cases). 'Every Frenchman has been, is now or will be Gaullist.' Between them and us, the affair is one of signature, of language. They have irradiated us all.

The hecatomb of 1914–18 left us no particular style. It is as if that enormous event had remained mute. It does not speak to us because it has no accent. It is an ocean of mud and blood, a mass of absurd and pointless heroisms, which leaves us disheartened and bleak of eye. The spirit becomes bogged down in it. There is little food for thought in the First World War, and still less to dream about. It is impossible to look at it and discern a pug-mark, the imprint of some individual will. There is nothing there but a vast combination of grinding and pounding mechanisms. The grandeur of a period is to be measured not by the scale of the events of which it is made – Great Revolution, Great War – but by the combination of a given quality and a given volume, something intense and something enormous. Napoleon and de Gaulle *styled* Europe's tragedies in a French manner, like Churchill from an English, and Luther or Bismarck from a German, point of view. By means, of course, of an exasperating exercise of will. But beyond that, by a way of writing what happened, or rather transmuting, rewriting the event into a super-event capable of replacing the truth. But they were not superimposing an aesthetic on an adventure (something that any tyrant, dictator or Führer can do); they were not just styling or decorating yet another enterprise of domination. Artists of this type incorporate style into their very action, whose effectiveness depends on things being done with a certain singularity. They transform a temperament into a factor of power.

Both these monuments are too lacking in private crevasses and fault-lines to resemble 'romantic heroes'. They are too marmoreal, too monotonous, for that. The souls of these monoliths can be found entire in their actions. Nevertheless, in our minds Napoleonic France and Gaullian France have become Napoleon's romance, and de Gaulle's; their many real personalities seem like characters the authors have arranged around themselves. Each captain had, if not a fluent pen, at least ready words. Vast quantities of ink – the very best ink – flowed around, with, for and against them. Napoleon has less talent than Chateaubriand, de Gaulle less talent than Malraux; but without the former, the latter would not have been such good writers. An epoch, like a farm or a child, belongs to the person who cultivates it. Our two cardiac stimulators quickened the pulses of millions of adolescents. They did not fascinate their successors so much as fashion them without their knowledge. Attempts are made to settle old accounts with these men of the past, as if discharging a duty, by putting up monuments and sticking their names on squares and airports. What we forget is that they have modified our outlook, our way of seeing, from the inside. Without knowing it, all of us, Frenchmen and Frenchwomen over forty, are minor characters in a work of fiction beyond our understanding; characters, incidentally, whom the novelist de Gaulle did not think worth developing. It seems we were not up to it.

Politics becomes serious when it mobilizes the imagination. All periods admit a certain amount of romanticism to public life. A lot of politicians could figure in *La Comédie humaine,* but very few give the impression that they are reinventing it. Individual talent is enough to create a resemblance to the young Rastignac, but to produce a Balzac history needs genius: exceptional circumstances have to offer themselves to an exceptional man. The history of France had genius in 1789 and in 1940. It is not something available to order. De Gaulle was quite correct when he wrote in *Le Fil de l'épée:* 'Nothing can be done without great men.' But he was wrong when he added: 'And they are great because they wanted to be.' For once Napoleon could have given him a lesson in modesty. 'A great man', he acknowledged soberly, 'results from the encounter between a great character and a great accident.'

*

Nothing ever turns out as badly as people fear, or as well as they hope. Napoleon and de Gaulle are rightly regarded as embodiments of will in politics. Great historical shocks push character to centre stage and jostle 'goodwill' into the wings. But the will of these two voluntarists was carried through against their wishes. Until 1815 Napoleon wanted a return to the Ancien Régime, for entirely personal reasons, without realizing that he embodied an idea larger than himself: legal equality of the citizens – in other words, the revolutionary individualism of which this parvenu was to be the vector in Europe, effectively giving rise to the modern individual. Until 1969 de Gaulle wanted France to have a free hand in an autonomous, adult Europe, but his efforts resulted in a France trimmed into alignment with the Community, a supposedly 'political' Europe which does not even dare to have its own policies. The champion of a Europe of peoples laid the groundwork, in effect, for the Europe of commissions. The irony of history turns our enthusiasms over like pancakes ... these days, leaving the Community seems tempting: what is the good of all this clamour? In the final analysis, what does will achieve?

But the Emperor, who was not a very pleasant individual, receives a hundred thousand visitors a year under the gilded dome of the Invalides. While the General, who respected people's rights, slumbers anonymously in a dilapidated country cemetery where no tourists venture. The true nature of a head of state emerges posthumously, and true grandeur can also be measured after death by an ethic of its own. This might be called modesty.

*

The chronology of our feelings is as enlightening as their intensity. 'Love for Napoleon is the only passion that remains to me,' noted Henri Beyle* in his late diaries ('which does not prevent me', he added, 'from perceiving the defects and miserable weaknesses of his mind'). Left-wingers of the last century – Stendhal is a good example – seem to have passed through three stages in their

---

*(*Trans.*) Stendhal.

feelings about Napoleon: admiration for the booted Jacobin, the victor of Marengo; hatred for the despot; veneration for the exile. After St Helena, and with Louis-Philippe on the throne, the republican Stendhal went back to his first love. In 1837 he wrote a *Vie de Napoléon*, the assessment of a character by an intelligence. The course of events might have given new employers to the Consul of Civittavecchia, but they could not withstand the inevitable comparison. 'In others one always finds something hypocritical, woolly or exaggerated that kills one's admiration at birth.'

Left-wingers of the present period have followed the same manic-depressive cycle in relation to de Gaulle. After admiring the leader of Free France, and detesting the 'factionalist' of May 1958, they are edging back towards an inevitable devotion to the father of the Fifth Republic. I even know disillusioned or frivolous individuals who murmur that love for de Gaulle is now the only political passion that remains to them, unaware that Stendhal has said it already.

Our national carbonaro went pretty far in his own defence. In the first edition of *Rome, Naples et Florence* he described himself as a former cavalry officer 'who ceased to be French in 1814'. Thinking over his Italian campaigns after Waterloo, he confessed that 'sooner or later, where military glory is concerned, one comes to have most admiration for great things achieved with small means'. I do not know anyone who handed in his passport in 1969, thank God, but I have since heard eminent observers deplore, where diplomatic strategy is concerned, the smallness of the things achieved by France in spite of its great means (especially military ones). That said, though, I think citizen Stendhal an irresponsible dandy for running off to play the émigré in the backstreets of Milan. A country does not die just because it takes a rest after making a bid for the summit. It is all a matter of rhythm.

4

The power of the word

'I treat scholars and wits like flirtatious women,' wrote Napoleon to his brother Joseph. 'You have to see them and converse with them, but you do not have to marry them or make them ministers' (8 January 1807). De Gaulle followed this good advice: he was careful not to take Simone de Beauvoir as a mistress. But he did not persecute her very much either, unlike his predecessor with Madame de Staël (despite the low-cut dresses she wore for the First Consul's benefit). Napoleon – who once distractedly, in a corridor between meetings, exchanged a few words with Goethe because 'one has to see these people' – would never have given Monge* a ministry or placed Chateaubriand on his right at Cabinet meetings. This macho Corsican repugnance for the vapid weaklings he called 'wits' is specific to the Emperor. No such vulgarity is apparent in the General, although like any pragmatic bourgeois or officer he despised phrasemongering, long-windedness and dogmatism. In his case, though, it was as much for moral reasons as for reasons of state. Napoleon feared intelligence as such, as a challenge or a threat; de Gaulle respected it too much to tolerate the characteristic irresponsibility of those we call 'intellectuals'. These privileged people believe that the way an idea aligns with reality is not a decisive measure of its value. And these days they

---

*(*Trans.*) Gaspard Monge, Comte de Péluse, mathematician, a founder of the École polytechnique.

possess a sovereign, recognized right to be in error, justified by their control of the University, with its innate authority. It is a fact that they would rather think about justice than think justly. A statesman cannot afford this luxury: he pays cash for his errors.

Both Napoleon and de Gaulle had ostentatiously bad relations with 'everything that swarms, intrigues or scribbles',* a phrase that seems to reduce us all to the level of copyists. This, of course, is a defect of strong governments. When Caesar is at his peak, Cicero is always at a nadir. Lawyers everywhere flee before generals, and vice versa. This immemorial seesawing between the state and the intelligentsia, reaffirmed throughout French history, is not a sufficient explanation in itself. De Gaulle, for a start, had a literary rather than a scientific background. Bonaparte, by contrast, was an artillery specialist and a good geometrician (a standard 'problem' bears his name); he was disdainful of littérateurs, but took the trouble to have himself elected to the Exact Sciences section of the *Institut* as a scientist, and during the Directory he assiduously cultivated distinguished fellow mathematicians. The *Institut* was still a hotbed of republicans at the time; hence the suspicion. 'Ideologue', in 1800, meant Jacobin, in the same way that 'intellectual' in 1960 meant 'left-wing intellectual'. The first conspired and fired off epigrams in the salons; the second brewed trouble and signed petitions in the papers. It has to be said that in neither case was the political context especially helpful. To make things worse, the unfrocked Jacobin Napoleon nourished the customary hatred of his former comrades, while pursuing the victorious assault (started by the Revolution) of science against the humanities. De Gaulle did not have these motives for rancour. He had done no avoidable damage to the cause of conservatism, and moved comfortably in the environment of the humanities.

This explains his – apparent – indifference to men of letters. He addressed Sartre respectfully as 'Cher Maître', ignored impertinent sarcasms, and went quietly about his business.

In reality, the universe of words was his true home.

*

---

*(*Trans.*) 'tout ce qui grouille, grenouille ou scribouille' (de Gaulle).

'*Legenda*' means in Latin 'the things that should be read'. Napoleon and de Gaulle are legends made flesh: word-men, narrative-bodies. Creatures of the tongue, effects of vocabulary. Both were masters of propaganda. Corporal Painting and General Microphone both pursued their aims through a highly organized propagation of messages, paying close attention to numerous matters which were generally thought secondary at the time: support, targets, circulation, 'special effects'.... Information media were routinely interposed between them and their contemporaries: *Bulletins de la Grande Armée*, the BBC, *Le Moniteur* and television, harangue before the massed ranks, soundbite for journalists. Things said and repeated, to be read and seen: legend in the raw. At a distance, a great deed can be confused with a *bon mot* and a breach of the line with a stroke of good luck. 'Soldiers! Twenty centuries are watching you ...'* 'France has lost a battle, but...'**

Propaganda can be defined as the art of managing one's legend. 'What a romance my life has been ...'† The master becomes his own masterpiece. His biography confers genius on literary talents and talent on political witnesses. But the master has worked on it himself, pen in hand, during his lifetime. Both men deliberately inserted text between themselves and posterity: here a *Memorial*, there some *Memoirs*. To which are added the writings of the professionals. Stendhal and Hugo, Balzac and Béranger 'did' Napoleon, as Malraux and the Mauriacs (not forgetting Bernanos and Pierre Jean Jouve) 'did' de Gaulle. There can be no doubt that the prisoner of St Helena had more luck with literature. The Gaullian legend was metamorphosed, amplified, by supporters whose credulity diminishes their credibility. Napoleon's was made by adversaries like Chateaubriand, people like Stendhal or Balzac who were not aligned with him, and by others like Hugo and Byron who did not take part in the events. This is more effective and less

---

*(*Trans.*) Napoleon in Egypt, speaking to his men beside the pyramids. 'Forty-five centuries' would have been more accurate.

**(*Trans.*) De Gaulle, 18 June 1940.

†(*Trans.*) Napoleon at St Helena.

suspect. In the long run, writers served the man who maltreated and despised them better than the one who always gave them respect.

Might not the injustice be repaired?

Nietzsche wrote: 'Napoleon, before whom even Byron was not ashamed to say that he was "no better than a worm beside such a being", has infused the soul of our century with that romantic prostration before the genius and the hero, which is so foreign to the rationalist spirit of the last century.'* The time has come to give the survivor from the nineteenth century the same right to transfiguration that served the product of the eighteenth. The artillery planner born under the Enlightenment, a classicist by inclination, resistant to dreams and dizziness, the cold positivist enamoured of the exact sciences, the very soul of dry abstraction, has ended up – with the aid of the romantic filter – haloed in an aura of upheaval and delirious excitement. A Prometheus shackled to his rock, chained by the ocean shore, crucified by Destiny, hostage of Kings . . . my eye! De Gaulle has a far better claim to this sort of scenic rearrangement. Take up your quills, little Byrons, switch on your screens! Snip and stitch among our living dreams. . . . Humanize this standing stone for us, put flesh on this neglected shade. . . .

Even if it means replacing our infantile daydreams of power – beyond our means and out of range – with an adult vision of dignity.

*

Napoleon was an oral being: he dictated his texts in the heat of the moment, starting with his *Mémorial*. A born writer, because he was spontaneous and impulsive, and in this respect more modern than de Gaulle. He comes on like Céline, de Gaulle comes on like Livy. The Emperor has the cavalier attitude to language of a man in a hurry. He treats it like a daughter; de Gaulle treats it like a mother: the *cavaliere servente* of an unattainable Lady. 'Mother, behold your

---

*(*Trans.*) Nietzsche, *Aurore*, aphorism 298.

sons who have fought so hard ...'* All this piety is damaging to style. There is a stale whiff of Oedipus about the pompous Latinist borrowings, the Alexandrines and ternary rhythms. De Gaulle as a writer lacks the judicious incompletenesses that stop the reader in his tracks. He survives by virtue of his outbursts, not his periods. *Quarteron, chienlit, Volapük*:** he is saved by his verve, made palatable by his gift of the gab. Napoleon has the literary advantage of never having learned French (indeed, his spelling was that of an errand-boy all his life). He was a 'primary', a geyser of rough drafts. De Gaulle was a 'secondary'. 'Everything', he used to say, 'that I do not write, I disown.' The one dictates, the other composes. A comparative study of their correspondences has yet to be made. It would be interesting, politically and in other ways. It would measure a telegraph against an academician, a voice against a style, a brutality against a courtesy – a horsewhip against a chisel.

It is not surprising that Stendhal, who could tolerate only what was natural, should have been Napoleon's hagiographer, and Malraux de Gaulle's. Chateaubriand would really have been more at ease with de Gaulle, for that specialist in afterthoughts, that echo-obsessive, loathed anything direct. His best passage on Napoleon was inspired by his death: 'So on 5 May 1821, at eleven minutes to six in the evening, amid the roaring of the wind ...' And for good reason: the news had taken *two months* to reach Paris, via London (Havas had not yet opened its news agency, and there were no electric telegraph cables across the Atlantic). By the time it arrived, ennobled by delay, with the added emphasis of distance, it was no longer news: it was already legend. The viscount was left with the task of writing an epilogue to an epilogue: an epitaph

---

*(*Trans.*) Charles Péguy.

**(*Trans.*) *Quarteron*: obsolete word meaning (1) twenty-five; (2) a quarter of a pound; (3) a (male) quadroon. *Chienlit*: a filthy and uncontrolled person (literally, shit-in-bed), hence general mess, botched occasion or project. *Volapük*: a universal language invented in 1880 by Johann Martin Schleyer; a predecessor of Esperanto. Volapük means 'world-speak' in Volapük. None of the words is in common use, and the second is surprising on the lips of a correct statesman like de Gaulle.

squared. Poor communications facilitate the sublime.

The aggrandizement of the subject *on the hoof* (so to speak) is
rendered even more meritorious by the absence of perspective.
Honour, then, to Malraux, who transfigured AFP dispatches into
an epic. Working over events as they happen makes the enthusiasm
more perceptible, and widens the margin of error. The account
(in *Les chênes qu'on abat*) of de Gaulle, at the fireside, being given
an account of Che's death, is pure *Paris-Match* schlock. Here
genius lies in giving the ring of truth to a collage of dubious
assertions. The result is an astonishing book assembled from an
accretion of ridiculous ideas.

*

In his *Lieux de mémoire*, the historian Pierre Nora aligns the three
key moments of national unity, personified in founding texts, with
Louis XIV, Napoleon and de Gaulle:

> The three men who embody national legitimacy most intensely
> in our history and mythology, who presented strong images of
> the State in the aftermath of the great crises that threatened its
> destruction – the Fronde, the Revolution and the defeat of 1940
> – all found themselves, under very different conditions and for
> apparently unconnected reasons, each writing in his own
> fashion a Memoir to set his image straight and give an account
> of his actions.

Let us examine this idea further. It stems from something
specifically French, which until recently was traditional, obligatory,
but whose demise has now been announced by the Fondation
Saint-Simon: the *vital* connection between the political and the
literary. The state's strong periods in our country, coinciding with
the low tides of intellectual power, are the moments when writing
is at its strongest (intellectuals and writers are not synonymous). As
if the primacy of the political over the economic, of the state over
civil society, had as its corollary the primacy of the written over the
oral. The big businessmen who govern our societies today, who
more or less 'sponsor' the state, are all – Italians, Americans or
Frenchmen – men of words; but they do not write, they telephone
and send faxes. When they need to communicate with the outside,

they 'intervene' by means of interviews or interview-books; they may need to express themselves or comment on events in writing, but they do not need to play the writer. They have a very different relationship with the time – an immediate one, without heritage or posterity – and with language, seen as a simple communication tool rather than as a sacred, living conservatory sheltering the spirit of a community. They speak the language of influence, not evidence; of function, not memory. A realist knows perfectly well that the memory serves no purpose, that memoirs are useless too. De Gaulle was a realist influenced by Bergson (and to a lesser extent by Péguy). So he knew that memory, in its way, is more real than matter; that a state worthy of the name is more than a simple technocratic organization, a combination of materially and socially useful apparatuses and mechanisms. He knew that deep down, a state *is* a memory: a spiritual reality. So that writing Memoirs – which, admittedly, are not especially useful or much read – becomes a way of nourishing the spirit of a people, patching up the state, preventing it from coming to pieces. It is a barrier against oblivion and the law of the strongest; a way to maintain a living, active, collective singularity amid the rising tide of homogenization and necrosis. In sum, it is a way of preventing a government from degenerating along the line of least resistance into an administration, as the vital surge of an inspiring idea falls back into colourless bureaucratic management. This is the reason for the politician's solicitude (and the technocrat's disdain) for the words of the tribe, those guarantees of survival and anchorage over long periods of time.

A state that wishes to be a spiritual reality is condemned to register itself in a language. Because a language is not just an instrument but a living environment, the golden thread of a lasting and singular vitality. Words accumulate as one is added to another; but each new image or broadcast chases out the last. A state that perceived itself as a product of public opinion, the ephemeral reflection of transient interests, could march in step with images, peak-viewing spots, measured impact; with 'advertising effectiveness'. It would be the journalist-state, something very like the one taking shape right now, before our eyes: an unstable collection of demanding lobbies, each represented by an appropriate ministry. A single operation can privatize the right to speech, the public companies, radio, television, even the 'great and good' themselves – who thrust themselves aggressively into the news, scattering lightning interviews, tasty quotes, soundbites. . . . Short-circuited by the speed of information, devoured by immediacy, they fall victim to a generalized Larsen effect, a sort of feedback resulting from too great a proximity in time between the source of a message and the receiver. Because de Gaulle's legitimacy is the product of a 'call from the depths of history', he speaks past us, over our shoulders, directly to our great-grandchildren, in those impersonal and compact Memoirs 'in which Charles never appears', a repertory of state language so distilled and unchanging that it could serve for a dialogue between Retz and Tacitus, Saint-Simon and Machiavelli, Richelieu and Caesar (there is not much of Julius in *The Gallic Wars*, either). He does not make us privy to his 'share of truth'.* He constructs the past, word by word, brick by brick. These days we have the tendency, marked as we are by audiovisual standards of truth, to measure the authenticity of an expression by its degree of intimacy or spontaneity. But this distancing of the self, this supercilious tension, impart to literary edifices of this type (in which extremes of artifice bizarrely combine with a sort of naturalness) a consistency which is altogether different from the Memoirs of people like Poincaré, Vincent Auriol or Edgar Faure. They wrote to justify themselves; other, younger men wrote to put themselves forward. De Gaulle wrote in order to be; or rather – for he wrote as he was – to ensure, by spelling it out, that his own past would become part of the nation's collective being. The greater solemnity of tone expresses the different status of the project itself. From where does de Gaulle's writing derive, not its prestige, but its legitimacy? From the fact that it is necessary. He is a Proust of collective hope: the raw material of history is processed after the event, the role of the past increases with time, the essence of a country is a sequence of art works.

He does not say: reality takes shape only in the memory. He says:

---

*(*Trans.*) A reference to Mitterrand's personalized memoir *Ma part de vérité*.

the state has reality only through Memoirs, the living being of a nation is given body by the text. An action is not legitimate because public opinion approves it at the time: its value comes from its meaning, from its inclusion in the panoramic unrolling of a very long adventure.

What used to be called 'History' perhaps involved a delay in information – a time-lapse effect, as it were. It can start to take on form and substance only when there is a perceptible gap between the event and its record. Between the man and his mark.

'When history comes to be written, we shall see that ...' Sorry, comrade: but no. What need will there be to write it later, when all of it is already *on record*?

*

Bonaparte was only a brain, but de Gaulle was something more: a believer. You can say he was the less intelligent if you like. But it is not intelligence that makes an intellectual, in the best and truest sense of the word. If it means 'a man who orders his life in accordance with an idea', then Napoleon was not an intellectual, but de Gaulle was. Of course he did not enjoy playing with ideas, nor did he love ideas for their own sake; brio is the mark of the interpreter, not the creator. The great strength of this cultured man was that he had an obsession, and stuck to it. Something along these lines: France is a living being, worthy of love, among other living personalities with all sorts of names, which for the time being are called 'nations', and which are also to be respected because, like France, they all want to live their own lives. Possessing a ruling idea, without allowing it to become an *idée fixe*, is what distinguishes the believer (or the intellectual) from the juggler on the one hand and the fanatic on the other. You are probably – and I am for sure – fairly dissipated people, subject to distractions and attractions, blown hither and thither by the wind: cinema, theatre, drink, women, travel, novels, friends, follies, idiocies, and all the rest. The great man is *unified*. He may be rough and uncultivated, but he is a conceptual creature (remember: 'The concept is what restores the diverse to unity'*). De Gaulle was a

---

*(*Trans.*) Immanuel Kant.

manifestly *collected* being. 'There was nothing that he did not correlate meticulously with the whole system of his principles and strategies' (Chaban-Delmas). But he had nothing of the obsessional, the monomaniac or the paranoiac hugging his little secret idea in private. Penetrating the barriers of the time and of his entourage, he avoided the complacency that so regularly descends on holders of the supreme post (who instinctively look away from anything upsetting, helped by the courtiers who are there to maintain a cosy atmosphere). He was an inspired man who still managed to breathe. He always sought the way out (in other words, information), especially when it was unfavourable to his current crusade. One cannot imagine him shuffling the Trafalgar message out of sight among the papers on his desk, as Napoleon did to his great cost. Or treating German reunification as a mere economic blip. The right degree of openness – somewhere between too much (opportunism) and not enough (sectarianism) – is rarer, or more difficult, than people think. The visionary or ideologue subordinates events to his idea. The vote-seeker or conqueror subordinates the idea to the event and espouses the moment, or the territory, or public opinion. Occupying the palaces and ministries was not an end in itself for de Gaulle, but a means. When he had to choose between his palace and his dream – something that nothing and nobody forced him to do – he left without a moment's hesitation, alone, with his little idea intact.

This can be put another way: Napoleon was an adventurer, de Gaulle a militant.

He was also, and by the same token, the last West European statesman to take the power of the mind seriously. The man who entered history on 18 June 1940 through a declaration, who knew from experience that a word can unleash all kinds of actions for better or for worse, who always conceived doing under the horizon of saying: such a man could only deal as an equal with other men of words. Of this respectful attitude he gave many proofs, touching, archaic or cruel. Refusing to reprieve Brasillach* – on the

---

*(*Trans.*) Anti-Semitic intellectual and Nazi collaborator, executed during postwar purge.

grounds that writing is an action, and all conscious men are responsible for their actions – is a sign of high esteem for the dignity of the printed word. Giving the highest rank to André Malraux in all his successive governments – because it is history that has precedence over politics, not the other way round – honoured the function through the individual. There was certainly no immediate advantage: reviled by the intelligentsia, scorned by the students and opaque to Peking, Malraux was hardly an ideal choice for chatting up the youth or getting Johnny Hallyday on the platform. De Gaulle's practice of inviting newly elected academicians to lunch, his visits to the *grandes écoles*, were not trivialities. Acknowledging the reception of every signed book with a handwritten letter to the author is not just a courteous gesture. The pre-eminence of the mind is recognized again and again in ways that go beyond mere formality.

These old-fashioned priorities and kindnesses have fallen out of use. Why?

Power, in every period, speaks to power. Writers and thinkers no longer merit so much consideration for the simple reason that they are no longer social powers. Writers have become celebrities like all the others. It is just that they have been demoted from the Politics page to the Social Affairs page. They have access to the reception room, and the dining room if they are well known, with a frequency based on their print runs, audience or public standing, like any other star of the Paris scene, and strictly for purposes of decoration or publicity (when the press attaché thinks it useful). What they may say or not say is a matter of no moral or political importance whatsoever. Eighty-two per cent of those questioned in a 1981 survey said that the opinion of intellectuals on matters under public debate was of little or no importance. In another survey in 1989, only seventeen per cent said they would trust intellectuals to understand the stakes in society, against thirty-five per cent who said they would trust business bosses. The depoliticization of intellectuals in France makes one with their devaluation, and coincides with the demoralization of the state.

Not that it has lost its morale. The state has simply changed moralists. These days it finds its inspiration in the same place as its free puffs: among the admen and famous hacks who sit at the

Prince's elbow, in the appointed role of adviser-confidant-crony, replacing the writer or sage of earlier times. It is with the opinion pollster and media consultant that the politician talks seriously of serious things: image and election prospects. People of letters, witty and amusing, are kept for the evening's social events: you have to have them, it's the custom. Plus a *chef de cabinet* with a command of rare adjectives, better than the sort of thing a *sous-préfet* comes up with, as a sign of grandeur.

In reality the two spheres have divorced. Statesmen and thinkers no longer take each other seriously. They still make sport of one another, but are no longer really interested. Perhaps it is for the best: thoughts without consequence crossed with the smiles of politicians without thought.

Will the sudden arrival of Eastern Europe among us make a difference? Over there, writers, intellectuals and scientists are at the heart of things, as they were in France fifty or a hundred years ago. The question is to know which of the two mediaspheres will prevail; whether our frivolous scepticism will gain ground faster among them than their naive gravity among us.

Since cultural cross-breeding is always conditioned by the underlying balance of forces, the answer, alas, is all too predictable. Reform can come only from the inside.

5

The mediological state

of grace

A quarter of a century on, the poetry of Gaullism has acquired a
patina of antiquity, giving it (to the modern eye) a fabulous
prehistoric quality: just look at the charming wrought-iron hinges.
De Gaulle had the good fortune to coincide with a technological
interregnum: somewhere between electricity and electronics,
during a period when the pen and the sword coexisted bizarrely
with the transistor and the moon-rocket. But before Economy and
Finance* had taken precedence within the state from diplomacy
and the armed forces.

In the decade from 1959 to 1969 the reign of the telegraph (a
vertical, virile, public and republican transmission technology)
had ended, while that of the telephone (feminine, horizontal,
private and democratic) had yet to begin. We were at the
interchange between the two-piece telephone with crank handle
and the time switchboard, between the post office in every village
and the telephone in every home. Hegemony had slipped out of
the academic's grasp, but the star TV-presenter had not yet
captured it. De Gaulle made full use of the new tools of power, at
a moment when the old still had enough sap and conviction to
command respect from impatient snot-noses gravid with the
future. Between more-of-the-same and not-quite-yet there occurs a
sort of social levitation, a scent of spring in the air, an April of the

---

*(*Trans.*) i.e. the Exchequer.

spirit, equivalent to the feeling that prevailed when three-masters jostled steamers in our ports and oil lamps still supplemented gas mantles in our bedrooms. Our own time juxtaposed on an equal footing Picasso and strip cartoons; Sartre and Bardot; coal miners and computer engineers; the CGT and the CNPF; monthlies and dailies; the lecture and the interview. It was an interlude in which strange anachronistic things could be seen in France: a state. The ardent compulsion of the Plan. Ambassadors in cocked hats. Caïds in Marseille. Masters of thought. A military strategy. Chequered tablecloths in bistros. Brassens and Brel songs in prime time. Masters' degrees at the Sorbonne. A diplomatic service. Senior civil servants. Intellectuals' manifestos. People addressed as 'mon cher Maître'. Targeted and signed political outrages. There was a lot of other stuff as well, but not yet all of it. In those days artists were still recalcitrant to the market, literature resistant to the communications industry, ministers harsh with journalists. It was a godsend to have returned to power between the age of advertising and the culture of the image, when Dim tights were seen alongside Dubo-Dubon-Dubonnet and other traditional frescoes. Perhaps this gave the impression that de Gaulle as a person combined the very old and the very new. For the old had not yet submitted: the Old World had not knuckled under to the New, France had not bent the knee to America. Armed with the very latest means of diffusion, the old fogey farted sheets of flame. A word-maker, 'the jetsam of some obscure disaster', in a universe where it was already essential to lead off with figures (survey, readership, entries, print run, quota, ranking), a prophet's memorial planted like an oak tree in the middle of a TV studio where a statistic – generally false – would soon pass for an argument: he should have shrivelled on the spot under the weight of ridicule. Instead he was dynamic, forceful, competitive as the devil.

How could he have been? I must be dreaming. But no, look, there are photos, film clips. Records. This is not just an Épinal*

---

*(*Trans.*) A town in the Vosges, centre of popular imagery from the late eighteenth century.

print, a fable for schoolchildren. It has become the subject of theses, the object of research and analysis, a name borne by squares and avenues. Only yesterday it was having successes, growling, climbing into limousines, waving its arms. We have the evidence in snapshots, on films and tapes. This painter of the imagination, who 'worked' France internally, with closed eyes, was caught externally by the image-thing: camera, cinema and TV. The symbol has left irrefutable chemical and electrical prints. De Gaulle now haunts us not as a state portrait or an oil painting, but as a 'photographic document'. It has the poignancy of a past made present. It is possible not to believe in a full-length portrait; a photograph outflanks illusion, attests that there really was a person bearing the indicated name. He is there no longer, he will never return. But he existed. The certificates of reality are there. Napoleon is historical myth, de Gaulle is true hallucination. A metaphor can be made from these purely material data, a gift of the technical development of memorials (mountings for carved inscriptions). It fell to this veteran of the 1914 War to oversee the transition from theatre to cinema, from Edmond Rostand to Jean-Luc Godard, from word to image. Audiovisual Shakespeare: history comes into my kitchen as tragedy via radio and TV, which have not yet had time to turn it into the sort of comedy we all recognize. Traditional theatre, complete with footlights, plush curtains and authors' speeches, was adapted to the small screen by a contemporary of Sarah Bernhardt. The result was docu-drama as truth. The protagonist acted as chorus, de Gaulle played de Gaulle, a close-up of the giant made him accessible and familiar, in my own sitting room. This media-dramaturge, bestriding two mediaspheres at a time when the media and the dramas of politics still led separate lives, was thus able to take advantage of both of them, without sacrificing the hard to the soft, the cutting edge of actions and words to the law of the electronic smile. In sum, he combined the advantages of authenticity with those of representation. Accepted the virtues of modern instruments while rejecting their vices. For example, he used the telephone but did not allow it to use him. 'On principle I never telephone, with very rare exceptions; and nobody, ever, summons me to the instrument.' An allergy often found in the pre-telecom generations, but also one that suits a stoical morality in which the chief is supposed to be impassive (Mitterrand shares it). In 1936, Colonel de Gaulle had visited Léon Blum in his office to explain the urgent need for equipping six new mobile armoured divisions. The President of the Council had been unable to follow the argument, for he was constantly interrupted by telephone calls. A scene since repeated, on a more human scale, an infinite number of times in an infinite number of Paris offices. We all know, now, that a man of power and influence owes it to himself to be overwhelmed, harassed, by a dozen importunate bells and buzzers. The author of *L'Armée du métier* (a magnificent success, selling seven hundred copies) was certainly not an important man. He knew, however, that what is urgent goes through the telephone and what is important is put in writing. And that a state is in danger of dying when, at its highest level, the immediate drives out the future. The head of the Popular Front was a man of the written word, attentive to the written word, but distracted, pestered, pulled hither and thither; and all because he did not know how to turn a deaf ear to the ringing of his numerous telephones (especially the calls from the British Foreign Office).

To act on people's hearts and minds, de Gaulle tapped all the potency of television, without being trapped by its omnipotence. It was a miraculous adolescence of sound-image: the dynamic without the dictatorship (the chummy tone, the interviewer perched on the corner of the President's desk, the obligatory reply to the inevitable question, and so on). An acrobat's achievement that leaves you wondering how much is owed to the tightrope-walker's strength, and how much to the weakness of the communications technology.

*

When he took power there were a million television sets in France: people still had TV at home. When he left it there were ten million, and people were at home on TV.

Whence a certain change in manners and morals. The state is always a showbiz affair. But yesterday's theatre-state was a very different matter from the TV-state that exists today.

In the Republic of 1965, a minister about to travel abroad would send for his office director. '*Monsieur le Ministre*,' the official would say, 'there are eight seats on the plane. Have you thought about whom to take?'

'Right. Well, my two technical advisers who have been following this business. The Geographical Director from the Quai d'Orsay. Ask that historian, Whatsisname, he's been working on the region for the last twenty years and may come in useful. And that archaeologist, too – you know the one – in case we have time to visit Petra. OK, that's it.'

'Very well, *monsieur le Ministre*. Might I suggest, though, that it wouldn't be a bad idea to let people here know about the visit. Don't you think perhaps a journalist . . .?'

'Damn good idea. See to it, will you? If there's a spare place. Have a word with *Le Monde* and . . .'

In 1985, the same conversation would go something like this: '*Monsieur le Ministre*, there are twelve seats on the plane.'

'What do the press people say?'

'There are already reptiles on the spot, but we need to take at least two crews.'

'Right. Well. Antenne 2, three bodies. Gamma, that'll be two more. Don't TF1 want to send someone?'

'They came last time.'

'Their funeral. What's left? *Libération, Le Figaro*, the *Nouvel Observateur* and *L'Express*. . . . That's the lot, isn't it?'

'Might I suggest, though, *monsieur le Ministre*, that it could be useful for the adviser who follows this business in the office . . .'

'Damn good idea. See to it, will you? If there's a spare place, tell young Tartempion he's to come. Photogenic lad . . .'

President to the competent minister, 1965: 'I am being pressed to adopt a position on this matter. And I am wondering whether the cause is just. Whether it is really opportune. What do you think?'

'I believe it is, *monsieur le Président*.'

Long silence, then the President again: 'And how would public opinion take it, do you think?'

1985: same office, same problem: '*Monsieur le Président*, the available opinion polls are pretty clear. Public opinion would not understand . . .'

'Very well. Next item on the agenda?'

'This is the one the French are most worried about at the moment – BVA and Sofres both agree – so it should get a terrific response ...'

'So be it. We'll have to take an initiative on that one, then. Work something out.'

Official talking to his entourage outside recording studio after broadcast, 1965: 'Did the message come through? Did I really make myself clear?'

Same scene, 1985: 'Was I all right?'

'Terrific. You still had seventeen per cent of the audience at the end of the broadcast. The opposition last Sunday was down to eleven per cent. We're laughing.'

It was a very long time ago, the period when political meetings were not opened by Charles Trenet and closed by Malraux; when speeches during electoral campaigns did not begin on the dot of eight, after a spectacular cascade of lasers and decibels; when the Élysée Palace had one press attaché and one only, a humble, rarely seen figure consulted only *in extremis*. When candidates for high office were chosen for their vision of the world, not for the world's vision of them (A *book*? What on earth for? A book is all very well, but it's not the same as a decent cuttings file, is it? Get yourself seen, my dear fellow. Put yourself about). It was unreasonable in that 'communication' was believed to describe a set of *means*. It was regarded as a tool that might be used to pursue a political end, not as a living environment like water for a fish, an ultimate end and yardstick of all values. It is very naive, as well as obviously erroneous, to regard the *medium* as a means, a utensil or an accessory. We know now, since the appearance of mediology as an autonomous discipline, that it is something much more important than that, much weightier and more serious: a system for transmitting traces. If this were not so, the thought-function would not have been marginalized by the communication-function from top to bottom of the scale of institutions, starting with the Catholic Church, which treats its theologians no better than the state treats its scholars. But at the time, the time of Vatican II, it was still possible to behave as-if. A Pope could still impress people with the content of his encyclicals, rather than by kissing the tarmac at the bottom of the gangway. Or a president with the content of his press conferences, rather than through films on his family life and his country house. Style counted, certainly; but so did content.

Let's understand one another. There is nothing new about the vanity game. Squabbles over the privilege of the tabouret* in 1680, or the tyranny of ribbons in the 1890s, were doubtless every bit as comic as the scrum around the cameras and microphones in 1990. The criteria of credibility have changed, but no new mediasphere ever completely replaces the previous one, or wholly contains it. These things never produce a catastrophe; just displacements, reshuffles, even – and above all, eventually – renovation: a paradoxical resurrection of the old way. 'The showbiz society' is not the last word of the human spirit. We can say, though, that somewhere between its infancy and its decline there is a period – the one in which we are floundering at present – during which the image liquefies the imagination, the social the political (or the poll figures the will) and the message the mission. The television evangelist, by force of prime-time TV spots, eclipses the Bible. Everyone knows that when the value of a message is indexed on its bearer, promotion of the bearer spreads the message. It has become a cliché to point out that we know almost everything about political leaders (their children's names, their wives' tastes, their hobbies, holidays, peccadilloes, and so forth), except what they symbolize or stand for. These days, for example, it would be astonishing, if not materially impossible, to see and hear nothing of a former president of the Republic. If a head of state resigned as soon as his seven years were up, just for a bad opinion rating, we would assume that he was seriously ill. De Gaulle ended thirty years of history with a press statement of two sentences and went straight home, never once speaking to a journalist, appearing on television or allowing the most trivial 'impromptu' intrusion on his

---

*(*Trans.*) The tabouret was a folding stool used by those privileged to be seated in the presence of the king and queen.

retirement, until his dying day: 'I am relinquishing my functions as President of the Republic. This decision takes effect from noon today.' There can be no finer example of the sublime through abstention. So much nobility packed into so few words; and by a man so often accused of being florid and grandiloquent.... Thirty years later, in the swamp of our idolatrous logorrhoea, this laconic retirement still leaves one open-mouthed, like a prehistoric bison drawing in the cave at Lascaux.

A mediatized world is a world without surprises. Babble conceived to astonish soon subsides into a soporific drone. The eternal paradox of glitter: de Gaulle hardly ever played the Mourousi game,* so people did not have time to get sick of him. As a hopeless old square, people found him captivating. When he tried to play the winner by singing popular duets with a mediocrat, they lost interest and hung up. Theoreticians define the value of information in inverse proportion to its predictability. That, in a nutshell, is why the 'information society' takes the life out of information and reeks with boredom. All the current affairs programmes, late night, evening or Sunday lunchtime, delving 'behind the headlines' with a rolling cast of pundits and politicians, are much the same. Vocabulary: three hundred words. Sentence structure: subject, verb, object. Key concepts: young, friendly, creative, strong, modern, smart. *Nice.* Life, life, life: a go-anywhere idiom, a vade-mecum of governmental enthusiasm: an ammo pouch of zapwords. I offer a bet to any of our famous interviewers: give me your questions and the name of the person you want to interview, and I will provide a very accurate set of answers. There will thus be no need to bother a busy person (with substantial savings all round). Never having assimilated the rules (jinking and dodging, using catchphrases, nodding or winking, sticking to common ground, being solemnly vague) of the game (tiptoeing through the minefield to collect as many as possible of the potential audiences, all schools of thought, all socio-

---

*(*Trans.*) Mourousi is a heavyweight TV interviewer who has done a series of intimate chats with Mitterrand.

professional categories), de Gaulle still believed that everything was permitted: even thought, which upsets people. He thought it was all right to alienate a good proportion of the public, to wrong-foot the predictable. Today's buttonholing politics divide us. The man who most brought us together started his career as a divider – de Gaulle the separatist – and never hesitated to take sides, to back the grain against the tares. Which is better: mass media under the thumb of the regime, as then, or a regime under the thumb of the mass media, as now? (See above for typical response: 'Well *basically* neither, of course ...') The much-needed happy medium may conceivably turn up around the end of the century. Meanwhile, the fact is that a state domesticated by communications, with a language polished to a dull gleam of mediocrity and a mind smoothed by the avoidance of controversy, is a lot less appealing than communications domesticated by someone like de Gaulle, in which the droll and the unexpected were abundant. Nobody mentioned the 'political class' in those days. Thorez did not talk like de Gaulle or sound like Mitterrand. Everyone had his own voice, his own audience, his own language and accent. 'Politician', which now means a professional like any other – perhaps not the most respected – counted as an insult in those days. A certain immediacy of tone was permitted in the Forum (the sort of thing we find so attractive in a Balkan prime minister who has not yet learned the Prime Minister game). Mediatized competition, the escalation of platitudes, places the champions on the same level: at conceptual zero. By smoothing out the differences between politicians, it makes us indifferent to the whole profession. Indifferent to the point of nausea.

To the question: 'So what is a statesman?', put to him by the former minister Jeanneney, who visited him in retirement, de Gaulle replied: 'A man capable of taking risks.' The question now, in view of the constraints on communication, is whether a politician who takes risks is not a dead man. A clear and distinct idea is the worst danger imaginable. The mediatized catch-all seeks the indeterminate, the indistinct, ten irons in the fire, the more the merrier. But to think properly, to conceive, always means distinguishing, isolating a particular idea, choosing one iron rather than the others; it means losing votes. Suffering image-corrosion. Falling in the TAM ratings. (If you ask a minister whether he leans towards a democracy of democrats or a democracy of republicans, he invariably replies that he leans both ways, there is nothing to choose between them, he does not get the distinction, etc.: a professional communicator's reflex, masquerading as serious reflection.)

Our leaders are distinguished by a trait which is no longer distinctive: they do not say what they do and they do not do what they say. In the short and electoral terms, this doublespeak pays (that is what it is for). But soon it will ruin those it has fattened with followings and constituencies, the *nouveaux riches* of the new hypocrisy. This last is a strangely 'moralistic' term to use in describing a total social phenomenon belonging to an era. It is the hiatus between socialist principles and the administration of capitalism that puts the language of our ministers out of phase with their conduct. The divorce between theory and practice inherent in every projection of an ideology into the real world usually leads to 'painful revisions'. Formalized, solemnized and set down in texts. What we have these days is no profound debate and no clear conclusion. There are no written references, just the minutes of formal transactions between bosses. Social security, lay education, taxation, arms sales, privatizations, control of the electronic media, European 'production quotas': everywhere a remorseless, gentle withdrawal, between the lines, behind a smokescreen of the unsaid, without any hint of what is being abandoned ever allowed to appear. Laying down your arms without an armistice, surrendering with flags flying: an original idea in the history of the twentieth century – already somewhat cluttered with capitulations – which doubtless owes a good deal to what the communication society calls 'transparency'.

The advertising-style management of the public domain plays down changes of course by spotlighting the faces in close-up. Abundant communications make dissimulation easier. We have a right to ministerial confidences, and to decisions carried through by legerdemain. True speech and woolly ideas are washed up on the same tide. Does it seem outlandish to evoke the contrast with the frankness, the brutality, of de Gaulle's interventions and way of speaking? Whatever might have been said about his skill in decoy tactics – notably in dealing with the Algerian *pieds-noirs* and in the field-messes of the Aurès* – double language was definitely not his forte. He was a good actor, they say. But a pathetic recruit for Diderot's paradox.** It seems that this man who carried his own double on his shoulders, like Aeneas Anchises, who referred to himself in the third person, could not be dismantled. He was all of a piece, the pachyderm: leathery emotion, gong-like feeling. Since his time we have been treated to excellent disrobing scenes – called '*L'Heure de vérité*',† 'The Moment of Truth' – for never is more *truth* (defined by what Lévi-Strauss elegantly calls 'the care it takes to dissimulate its presence') spoken than in these tinpot documentaries. Not much is said, but it is always said with a smile, and in front of a grand audience whose presence confirms the value of the champion under the spotlight (like the pretty girl whose presence in an advertisement reassures us that the coffee-grinder will work properly). 'You think I have no aims? You can see that I have associates.... My programme is this unprecedented range of celebrities. Who can say more?' When the state is confused with society at large, law with customs, right with deeds – when, in other words, the imported notion of 'civil society' has supplanted the revolutionary notion of national sovereignty – then the people becomes confused with the population and the ruling elite can convince everyone that it is making policy by appearing on chat shows. This is called 'people-orientated' government. 'The state is not a matter of contacts,' de Gaulle used to say. It is hard to imagine *him* assembling a platform of celebrities or appearing on TV behind a rat-pack of star supporters: Johnny Hallyday, François Mauriac, Françoise Sagan, Brigitte Bardot, two or three industrialists, etc. Nobody ever expected *his* radio or TV homilies to be interrupted by twenty-second spots for Lustucru and Pepsi. Before this simpering and ingratiating cordiality could become

---

*(*Trans.*) i.e. the army in Algeria, which generally supported the settlers.

**(*Trans.*) Diderot's paradox: that an actor who wishes to express an emotion does so more effectively if he does not actually *feel* it.

†(*Trans.*) 'Searching' TV interview series with politicians, stars, etc., similar to, for example, 'Face to Face', 'The Frost Interview'.

our daily portion, it was necessary for the state to allow itself to be swallowed by society, for the deed to stand in everywhere for the right (like sociology for philosophy), and for the general interest to be reduced to the sum (obviously impossible to calculate) of individual interests. It was necessary for the reappearance of great men to strip the state of its own grandeur. It was necessary for the political, in the sense of a distinctive power, to abdicate before the French exception could align with the European average, to loud cries of praise for modernity, openness, competitiveness. It was necessary for the feeling of inferiority to a rich and victorious America, which seized the average European after the war, to reach the average Frenchman; for the bottomless obsequiousness of the European ruling classes to become the yardstick of the 'European spirit' under cover of 'political co-operation' in the Community.

The crucial turning point was the day the TV weather bulletin stopped being presented by a meteorologist. The day the 'Weather Man' became a person who read the isobars off a teleprompter instead of one who drew them on a map. This switch occurred somewhere around 1968.

As for the passage of cyclones, so for the passage of time. In history too, saying was substituted for doing. In the quarter-century between Malraux and Decaux, the great biographer found his way on to the great man's throne. A history that is recounted has succeeded the history that used to be invented. Once an actor-country, France has become a witness-country of world history. It has placed itself in a showcase, and is gazing at itself with bleary eyes. Once it was a player on the stage, erect and somewhat impulsive; now it sits reasonably in the auditorium, warm and comfortable but moved at the sight of the world's upheavals, so reminiscent of its own past, the youthful follies of 1789, 1848, 1944.... We call this change from presence to representation a 'return to reality'. We are smug about it. France has given up picking quarrels with windmills. It has left its arrogance in the cloakroom. De Gaulle was a lunatic, mad enough not to take images of things for the things themselves.

He had the history disease. We have the 'museum sickness'. In the absence of an aesthetic the era has invented 'museology', and our semiological sophistication compensates for the enfeeblement of the signs. There are more CDs and a wider choice of performers, but less music is made at home, in the evening, among the family. Since his time a sort of celebratory and commemorative inflation has replaced the moody hero and old-time genius with fanciful exhibitions and fabulous processions. Yes, we have placed the imagination in power. But we are still not the vanguard. We are conservatives. Lacking matter, we work in manner. We are looking after our heritage, we are opening a museum a month in France and even, in Paris, a museum of museums, with a catalogue of catalogues. Alain Cuny, in *Tête d'or*, drew my time for me as it unfolded; now even the strip cartoon has its museum at Angoulême, and it is extraordinary. So protected and theorized have our 'historic sites' become that our historians now see the very Republic as a charming and preposterous mythology. We are the Restoration of the Monarchy, Mark 2. That was the time, after the revolutionary epic and the Napoleonic depletion, when the notion of heritage made its first appearance with the invention of the Inspectorate of Historical Monuments, the School of Palaeography and Librarianship, the Society of Antiquaries. A time that placed Guizot, Mérimée and Viollet-le-Duc on a pinnacle, as we place our historical school and our restoration projects. That was when the past became the past. It is only when history empties that it fills up with historians. But 'for de Gaulle, history was not some museum to be visited. It was integral to the flux and development of nations, present in its totality at every moment of its existence.' It is we who are the traditionalists, believing as we do that there is such a thing as anachronism, that the past does not inhabit the present. De Gaulle, a contemporary of the permanent, did not bother with these distinctions. He understood what we find so difficult to explain: the co-presence of different times, involving us mysteriously, willy-nilly, in things like religious wars or the invasion of the Palatinate. A man of history moves, without thinking about it, in thought, if this word is taken to mean all that establishes a link between the past, the present and the future. Time as punctuality – the triangulation of 'events' – has now sidelined History as an organic whole. The Left in power – the Left of country houses and palaces – has reduced it to an essentially decorative practice, as a backcloth to its media presentations: Summits in the Gallery of Mirrors at Versailles, Cabinet meetings in châteaux on the Loire. It looks good in the picture, but a picture is all it is. It is possible to imagine a dialogue between Malraux and Jaurès, or Malraux and Barrès; but not between them and us. Culture as drama has nothing to say to culture as production. It would be like a river conversing with an aquarium. With reality, of course, overwhelmingly on the river's side.

So the 1968 prayer has been answered, and de Gaulle is in the museum. And we . . . we form a docile queue, tamely cough up the price of admission and wander in to gawp. Each at his post, each in his spot. A couple of notches out of adjustment, mediatized, half-aesthete half-voyeur, we quite enjoy the images of other people's mayhem, before turning back to our own images, which are live and in colour. As if consoling ourselves for losing our hold on events with an unprecedented profusion of luxurious simulacra, in this Europe of tomorrow of which France talks better and better as it counts for less and less.

6

Return of the great man

Democracy loves mankind. It does not love great men. The one because the other.

The refusal to delegate, the insistence on autonomy, are its driving force and its pride. Greatness is for all, and popular sovereignty cannot be embodied in a single individual without being confiscated or – worse still – surrendered. Philosopher and jurist repeat in chorus: Woe to the people that has need of heroes!

To acknowledge the great man is to accept that the rest of humanity, $n-1$, may be small. Consenting to this diminution helps to perpetuate it. Democracy wishes all men to take charge of their destiny, as equals, and to amplify one another in the process: a cumulative and reciprocal greatness belonging only to the collective and called Party, Class, Nation or Humanity.

So speaks, in each of us, the vicarious chimneysweep. It is more than a hundred years since the children of Rousseau and Marx were crying from their makeshift platforms: 'Neither God, nor Caesar, nor Tribune.' We believe in salvation, we do not want a Saviour. We have an evangelist, but find Apostles suspect. Whether the principle is yesterday's 'History is made by the masses' or today's 'The world is led by ideas', professions of faith by the Left are always officially declined in the plural. While the Right, believing that a flock without a shepherd is a stampeding mob, has always *personalized* the debate.

Start with the appellations: Socialists versus Gaullists, a contest between followers of an idea and followers of an individual.

Look at our celebrations: 18 June carries a person's name, 1 May does not. The history of the Right is a portrait gallery, that of the Left a succession of crowd movements. French Revolution, the June days of 1848, Commune, Popular Front: these uprisings have no face, or several. The French workers' movement resembles a collective biography (Jean Maître's history of it takes up thirteen volumes); the history of traditional France a succession of hagiographies (Saint Louis, Richelieu, Louis XIV, etc.).

The national parties were supposed to have leaders, and the workers' organizations were supposed to have administrations. Evolved Stalinists used to refer to the management by names like executive group, team, nucleus and central group (at a time when the Comintern called itself 'the international headquarters of the party of the world proletarian revolution'). Although in practice the two always converge after a while, Communism is based on dictatorship of the apparatus, fascism on that of the saviour. Our historical maladies reveal our respective sins.

What could be finer than the protest of the Geneva Internationals in about 1873, against being called Marxists, Bakuninists or Lassallians:

> The very act of grouping sections around the names of individuals is a deplorable deed, contrary to our principles and to the cause of workers' emancipation. Self-regard, pride, ambition, all the passions inherent in the human personality, are being substituted for the general interests of the masses. People are forgetting the slow, cold, continuous and methodical action necessary for these interests, and getting worked up for or against this or that individual, whose elevation or downfall is always easier to bring about than a bit of progress or the elimination of an abuse.

The text adds:

> These personalities are seldom workers; they are déclassé bourgeois, doctors, teachers, writers, students, even some capitalists. It is necessary to root out the cause of the evil as well as to change humanity. No more Marxists or Bakuninists. A real and sincere alliance of the workers.

But there was still a need to regroup, and thus to have a tag that distinguished them from their adversaries. And so the 'Marxides' were born, then the 'Marxians' and finally the 'Marxists': an epithet ridiculed at the start which soon grouped all the hirsute sage's putative sons.

A century later, no Paris socialist would dream of saying: no more Mitterrandists, Rocardians, Fabiusites. It would seem absurd to call for this intellectual or moral reform. Is this what happens when we have teams instead and in place of defunct schools of ideas? When socialism declines into a system of patronage? When there is upward social mobility in conduct and among the rank and file? All this is true, but not sufficient to explain everything. The root of the evil is to be found not in sociological variables, but in a constant of anthropology: everybody is somebody's son, and nobody gets his name from himself. A symbolic law. A man's identity, not just his civil status, requires the mediation of the Other. Something that is also true for 'an alliance of the workers'. Mirage or sleight of hand, legitimation by citing the name of the Master has become left-wing practice. A progressive rationalist would say he was a man by necessity and French by accident. But the same person would specify his political identity by naming the leader of a school or tendency. At one time this would have been a theoretician in Germany, or a tribune in France. These days it is someone photogenic and fluent, or a plausible future president. For the *aura* shifts as technologies mutate. The theoretician's audience, the warrior's glory, the strategist's authority, have given place to the leader's canned applause, but the one thing that has not changed for the valiant knights of the impersonal is being labelled with someone's name. Ideas do not stand up all by themselves and, group or individual, nothing is born with impunity.

A rule: he who would be an angel on behalf of the masses soon finds himself acting the beast under the orders of a boss. So the heirs of 'the workers' emancipation will be brought about by the workers themselves' were able to generate, or stomach, personality cults so barbaric that those of the Ptolemies, the Seleucids or the Caesars seem modest and bucolic by comparison. Would it not have been worthwhile to admit at the outset that a collective

47

ambition is not realized through collective elaboration, but is mediated by one or more individuals? When did a political programme ever originate from a party congress? A scientific discovery from an interdisciplinary seminar? A style of painting from a meeting of the Academy of Fine Arts? A collective comes into existence, either as something aware of itself or as the bearer of a historic project, only through the mediation of words, however unpredictable and subjective the process may be.

In the sixties the politicized young looked for their demigods abroad: Lenin, Mao, Castro, Ho Chi Minh. Their effigies filled the foreground and hid everything else. How were we supposed to realize that we had a great man in the house, within easy reach? After all, his hands were dripping with blood – the blood of Algerian patriots, of the Charonne victims crushed against a Metro ventilator by the police.* Seven dead, and a million demonstrators flooded the boulevards. At the same time Chairman Mao was making corpses by the million, and not accidentally either, without a single person demonstrating in Paris. The more ruthlessly we exposed the imposture behind every legend in France, the more trustingly we took legends in the Third World at their own valuation, without a glance at any dubious areas. We scrutinized the immediate social environment in terms of class, mass, social reality, but paid far more attention to the name-symbols of the 'proletarian countries' than to the social experience these names actually represented. It is well known that people who are squeamish about patriotism tend to espouse more powerful nationalisms: our Communists have long cultivated a Soviet nationalism, as our liberals have the American variant. More sincerely but in the same alienated fashion, proud of what should have shamed us and ashamed of what could have filled us with pride, we totemized the charismatic leaders of backward nations into pillars of world doctrines. For quite some time, I was a Third-Worldist; the messianism of the pre-industrial oppressed seemed

---

*(*Trans.*) The Charonne victims were Communists, accidentally crushed during a demo.

to me to represent something universal. I believed that progressiveness was embodied in the fusty archaism of rain-makers like Nasser, Sékou Touré and Castro, and held the Gaullists around me to be ignorant simpletons.

To make everything worse, it was the golden age of the 'social sciences'. From the up-to-date student of the time – a Marxist polluted by contact with Lévi-Strauss and Braudel, with a smattering of structural anthropology and *temps immobile* – anyone in France who might conceivably be saddled with the satirical title 'man of providence' would raise, at best, a pitying sneer. His own great men had set him at odds with Plutarch. If a mainstream Rousseauist holds that the hero is a usurper, a sound Braudelian sees him as a man simple enough for history as a sequence of battles between kings; to a structuralist he is a pure effect of misinterpretation. The truth about a society or period can be reached only by penetrating this surface glitter to rummage in the anonymous and the collective, the unconscious and the material. Or so the chatter made out. The works themselves were more complicated. Lucien Febvre, after all, had praised Luther and studied Rabelais. And did not Marx extol the Jacobins and bourgeois heroism? Who wrote: 'Ignoble souls do not believe in great men'? Jean-Jacques Rousseau.

In fact, the theoretical downgrading of the great man started long before the recent appearance of these soft sciences, whose primary weaknesses are so poorly concealed by their terroristic findings. It dates originally from Newton and Laplace. *Celestial Mechanics* reduced the world to a system in which every form is deduced from the laws. In the context of that kind of determinism, the great man is just a badly conceived equation. He violates the principle of causality. There is no place for the singular or the contingent in a rational universality that conceives the physical and historical universe as a collection of orderly, stable, reversible systems. So the hypothesis of the 'great man' survived in the Enlightenment world as a naive or eccentric throwback to the Graeco-Roman ethos, until the new paradigms of reason replaced its intellectual scaffolding and restored it to relevance. Probability analyses applied to situations of irreversibility (turbulence in hydrodynamics, for example) restored singularity, fluctuation and uncertainty to respectable status. A sequence of events may include identifiable points of bifurcation, at which an individual decision may alter the overall direction of things by amplifying some tiny fluctuation. So 'order through noise', latest theoretical tool of the life sciences, rehabilitates Alexander the Great. Without joining in the polemic surrounding what René Thom calls the new popular epistemology, without calling on such notions as 'strange attractors' or 'ruptures of equilibrium' for purposes of apologetics, one can certainly say that a theory of chaos has taken shape (which one day, perhaps, will restore meaning to a whole category of outmoded formulae: if Robespierre or Carnot had not been there in 1793, the French Revolution would have lost its war against Europe. If Churchill had not been Prime Minister in London in June 1940. . . . If de Gaulle had not been in France in August 1944. . . . If Gorbachev had not been in the Politburo in 1985 . . .). We are beginning to understand how the insubstantial can triumph over the substantial, Solzhenitsyn can overthrow the Czar, and the beat of a butterfly's wing in the middle of an Australian desert can resound in the green fields of Erin 'perhaps tomorrow or perhaps in two centuries, in the form of a hurricane or a balmy breeze, according to chance' (Michel Serres). It took us much science and many centuries to refute the magical belief that the universe was governed by the whims of the gods, in the same way that human destinies hung on the pleasure of kings. Now it seems that the 'objective laws of history' may themselves turn out to be a residual myth from the dawn of the magicians, and that the ancient myth of the great mover may come to appear a subtle idea, prefiguring the high noon of a more exact reason. The half-scholar minimizes the role of the individual; the true scholar may one day rehabilitate it.

So rejection of the great man may have stopped being a sign of rigour and become one of conformism. How far do we really go along with it?

The republican is somewhat split on this question. As a layman, he makes a point of denying anyone's essential superiority over other human beings. Nothing and nobody can claim authority over him, evade the rules of free investigation or stand above the ordinary proofs of experience and understanding. The republican is an average man, who takes pride in the average and is suspicious of the arbitrary or the exceptional. But it is in his nature, physical and moral, to recognize and admire excellence. He is not really happy unless he has someone to admire (and/or unless he is in love). Just as the Tocqueville-style democrat feels humiliated by an indication of personal greatness, so the Rousseau-type republican feels exalted by it, as if the 'superior man' were there only to liberate others (himself included) from their inferiority.

We should accept the great man, but withhold ourselves from him. Yes to the image, no to the idol. Admiration without abdication: let's call it Rousseau's proposition, every bit as prudent as Pascal's. The position of the anticlerical believer.

It is true that in these parts, these fetishistic, apostolic and Roman regions, corrupted by the cult of saints, immaculate Virgins and sovereign Pontiffs, political beliefs can never be too Protestant. No human being shows the way to Heaven, no living human is the recipient of our prayers. Nothing and nobody is sanctifying in its own right, and all our works are equivalent in their vain pretension to the absolute. Never say: the Messiah has arrived, I know the true way, follow me. Any third party who intrudes between God and humanity will produce hierarchy, intolerance and catechism: in other words, Church. Any third party who intrudes between the individual and the state will produce dogma, stupidity and cruelty: in other words, Party. And what holds for the institution also holds for the personality. If there must be a third party between the sacred and ourselves, if we have to give way on something to keep the rest, then let us at least keep the 'mediating ministers' on short commons: let us give them what is due to a *minister* (which means, among other things, a servant or domestic).

But then what a dispiriting wilderness it would be, a state without images or effigies, without references or 'great figures'. Without anybody to admire. It would be slow death by suffocation.

De Gaulle's figure makes me deeply unhappy. He is dead now, but I am still living; and during his lifetime I never paid my respects. I never even *saw* him.

That said, I want to add straight away that de Gaulle fills me with happiness. It is so comforting to think that he was alive among us. For a long time to come, his name alone will serve as a giant India rubber to erase mediocrity.

In this ambivalence of feeling, comfort finally predominates. The bitter regret is real enough – the repeated farewells that can never be final, the feeling of a rough game in which I have been badly mauled. But the fallen star is a beacon for others to come. The Republic will see others one day. The sky is not empty: it is just that there are gaps between the stars.

*

We should look for an India rubber. We should ask for image and butterfly's wing. See examples above. It would be feeble of us to abstain.

An idea without an image is a battle without a soul. A town without fountains. Can you think of an exemplary man?

The Left has lost its legends. It lacks plot. It inaugurates, unveils, transfers, buries with indefatigable zeal, but it has lost its memory. This introduces a major new twist into the psychological profile of the Left, and radically alters its rules of action. Every historian knows that the legend of the Paris Commune was more important than the event itself, in the evolutionary history of what used to be called the workers' movement. What are we modernists and postmodernists going to put in place of our vanished foundation myths, our utopias and colour prints? Perhaps nothing at all? That will make us the new apostles of immobility. The party of Order. 'Who needs pious images when there's work to be done? Everyone knows the losers are a bunch of junkies....' The people in the saddle have no time for ideas, and the only images they care about are their own. A pity really, because they must have been told that the much-deplored 'mechanical wear and tear' and haemorrhage of militants have something to do with the debasement of our heroic references, a famine of the exemplary that we feel in our bones.

The Left used to be a vocation. It has become a trade. The difference is that the imagination serves the first as a motor, the second as an ancillary. Militants used to be people like officers or Dominicans. People became White Fathers because of Père de

Foucauld,* or submariners because of Lherminier and his *Casa-bianca*.** They became revolutionaries because of Trotsky or Che Guevara. They had seen films and paintings, read biographies. Whatever people may claim, *for whom?* always came before *for what?* Collective models always live through examples. When asked, as a schoolboy, whom he would most like to be, de Gaulle replied: 'Cyrano'. And that was his nickname at Saint-Cyr. In whose footsteps do you think people today should become socialists? Those of some deputy, well known, well off, protected by an official amnesty ...? Don't make me laugh. That is called scraping the bottom of the barrel.

Socialists should stop lying to themselves, and recognize that their Pantheon is full of skeletons. Their names are trotted out from the platform at the beginning of every congress, with a piety that tends to flag when the TV cameras are not running. People do their best, but their hearts are not in it. Our tutelary shades lie buried in silt. Nobody is going to make the slumbering militants dream with tales about Gambetta in his balloon, or the proconsul Clemenceau grappling with ministries and shooting strikers (his career as 'the Tiger' is not really our business). Léon Blum, though, counts as family. An eminent, respectable great-uncle, disinterested, acute, persevering and accessible. As a Councillor of State he heads the chapter entitled 'Morality and Politics', but this will not be the most important chapter in future history books. Fascism is not vanquished with non-intervention, and state power is not won with good editorials. He saw far and accurately into his century as editor of the *Populaire*, and into literature as a critic in *La Revue blanche*. Blum was the first to predict the fall of Lenin, while October was still at its height. He was a pure Marxist who gave democratic socialism an axis and an identity. But the war

---

*(*Trans.*) Father de Foucauld was a missionary and Saharan explorer who built a chapel and refuge at Assekrem near Tamanrasset in southern Algeria. He worked among the region's Tuareg nomads, wrote treatises on the Tuaregs' Berber dialect, and was murdered, probably as the result of a misunderstanding, in 1916.

**(*Trans.*) Submarine commander who fled Vichy France with his craft to join the Free French forces.

swept away, and its aftermath embalmed, that just man ennobled more by intelligence than by character. The aristocratic socialist, the dilettante of action saved by his faith in Humanity – Humanity is God – suggests the image of a foundering hero, holding his head high in adversity but failing to surmount it.

All these reference-names project well above the tree-line. How is it, then, that they arouse respect but not fervour? How is it that our own top achievers do not show above the skyline, either? That there are *Cahiers Léon Blum* but no Blumist movement? That avenues and metro stations are named after them, but they are never seriously considered for the place de l'Étoile? Is it because none of them achieved supreme power? Because they left no durable institutions? Because they were so long ago? No. The illustrious, at a distance, take on the scale of our dreams. And these illustrious men no longer make us dream.

There is still Jaurès. I would like to think that he is still part of our heritage. But he certainly has no hold on our imagination. He lacks support there, for technical reasons: his trace resembles a faded office memorandum, wholly literal, without any analogue component. There remains no clue to this man, no imprint. Almost no sound or visual record. Abel Gance made a film about Napoleon, but no director has shown any interest in Jaurès. Perhaps because he did not become an *image*. He is a *symbol*, something elitist rather than popular. The silver-tongued Saint Jean Bouche d'or of French socialism speaks truths, but in abstract dead language (witness his thesis in Latin, *De primis socialismi germanici lineamentis*, which nobody can read nowadays). There are at least two radical breaks between the universe of an 1880 academic and our own day: one is cultural, the disappearance of the 'humanities'; the other is mediological, the arrival of sound and image. Jaurès is a great name, but that is all he is, alas. We could really do with this crucial elder, a man who went beyond Marx before Marxism even existed, blending reform and revolution, republic and socialism. But he did not become a living and active myth, for the paradoxical reason that he gave his life to a myth, the Workers' International. Like Rosa Luxemburg, like Kautsky – even Trotsky himself, despite his adventurous brush with destiny – he is a man not so much of history as of an idea of history that – as it happens – has not been embodied. The rare sepia shots of the great little man, bearded, bowler-hatted, attached to the red flag and to our utopias, exude the pathos of the future perfect: here is a man who is going to give his life for something that will not have happened. No doubt our national prophet of a workers' dawn that ended in blood and boredom was saved by his murderer from the two moral humiliations between which he would have had to choose after August 1914: the *Union sacrée* and exile to Switzerland. He has since inhabited a void between the Republic he was born too late to embody and the socialism he died too soon to invent. Relative freedom from discredit is an advantage of failure. Jaurès did not decline, like Lenin. He has dried up on the stem, a tough faded poppy laid on the tomb of French socialism.

The Right conjugates its visions of paradise in the past tense. The Left's romanticism of the future is something more fragile: to stay on top of its present it needs reference-points and signposts, either in the past or in some utopian oasis, some fantasized but tangible China. Why do we have this feeling of emptiness? Because all the bridges have been cut between a disembodied ideal of the future whose outlines remain wholly obscure, and the founding myths we now think irrelevant. Jaurès's grandchildren, too, find themselves between two stools: between a purely technocratic futurism and the lugubrious rhetoric of their legends.

7

A visionary among

the myopic

There is an irritating saw to the effect that history is tragic. But it is not tragic because it shackles human beings to the treadmill of war and suffering; they are immune from that only in UN homilies and the successive charters of their succession of Societies of Nations. The bloodshed factor, banal in itself and subject to endless scrutiny, merits only the epithet *dramatic*. The reason why history is *tragic* is that nobody understands the smallest part of it while it is happening; that people live through it without seeing a thing. The tragedy lies not in massacre but in misunderstanding. It has nothing to do with tears. Indeed, it more often wears a smiling face than a gloomy one. Fabrice at Waterloo* is a young man who is both light-hearted and perfectly tragic. The twenty-year-olds at the École normale in 1950, 1960, 1970, those professionals of the right idea and perfect timing, were just as cheerful, just as fit, quietly enthusiastic and filled with absolute certainty, when they found complexities where none existed. It is easy enough to admit it when twenty years have passed: the decent interval for admitting an error, the time it takes even the most lucid to call a spade a spade and recognize a 'revolution' as a fine and necessary balls-up.

De Gaulle, it seems, pretty soon resigned himself to 'the hostile

---

*(*Trans.*) In Stendhal's *The Charterhouse of Parma*.

coalition of committees and pen-pushers'. The country's electoral history and geography explain the hostility of the Centre–Left cassoulet. The anti-Bonapartism of the South-West, which gave rise to the Théodore and Hippolyte committees,* is an old and healthy tradition. But the frivolity of literary gents, and the pettiness of news hacks, do not wholly explain the disdainful attitude of the Sorbonne and the Paris press. Of course it is not in the nature of littérateurs to take risks supporting losers (see 1940); nor can newshounds, eyes glued to the telex, be expected to open their arms to millenarians. This is neat and to the point, but it does not tell the whole story. As if it were just a matter of Jean Cocteau and Pierre Brisson!** A lot of *artists*, including some of the greatest, supported that artist of action. But to explain why most French intellectuals, the best included (Kojève and a few others apart), should have perceived de Gaulle as a chaste Boulanger, or a Napoleon III intimidated by the masses, will take more than a few world-weary generalizations.

*

I belong to a generation that does not have blood on its hands, God (and the serenity of the times) be praised. It has generally been on the side of the angels. But it seems to me that the blunders it has committed deserve at least as much scrutiny as the crimes it has not. This is not a moral judgement – we have always been 'the' moral generation, there is a new one every spring – but a meteorological observation. It never knows what the weather is going to be like tomorrow. 'We are the generation of catastrophes,' said Captain de Gaulle in 1920 to a young Polish officer friend. Our generation of experts on the meaning of history could be described more modestly as the generation of misinterpretations. From 1945 to 1975, my guild professed as a scientific fact that class struggle was the motor of history, that the collapse of capitalism was inevitable, that the eventual appearance of

---

*(*Trans.*) Republican lay committees formed under the Third Republic, now seen as extremely old-fashioned.

**(*Trans.*) Editor of *Le Figaro*.

something resembling socialism – with workers' councils, self-management, socialist democracy, and so on – was inherent in the structure of things. On discovering their error (a simple error of foresight), most of them responded by espousing a new one, with the same energy, application and trenchancy they had devoted to the first. So that 1975 to 1990 saw a right-about-turn, a change of outlook: individualism is the predominant force of our time, Human Rights the motor of history and the development of Democracy inevitable. The lads are in for another disappointment. They saw European unification through rose-tinted spectacles, in soft focus, a post-Yalta apotheosis of buddyhood and human rights. How were they to know that the black would come so soon after the red? The priest after the commissar, the ethnic group after the Party? One would so have liked them to be right. What feeling socialist prefers hatred to brotherhood? What rational democrat has a taste for war and nationalisms? But look: we were wrong to imagine that if there was one group who could be relied on not to mistake their desires for realities, that group was the 'intellectuals'. Even though that was what they were paid for. Perhaps we do not pay them enough any more. Perhaps they are not given sufficient material ease to enable them to get a perspective on our desires, to distinguish calmly between true and false. They want to be paid off on the spot, in immediate social recognition. *Then* they will work to order.

It is an advantage of rushed societies, whose pace is set by the traffic speed of messages and goods, that scholars can make more and more mistakes without their authority suffering in the least. In fact it matters less and less, for our accomplices the journalists do not read anything. Theirs is the decisive voice on the floor of the Prestige Exchange, and they happen to be people who have time for only a quick gulp here and there. Because to read, *really* to read, means to reread; and rereading takes time. Try asking the flurried presenter of a TV culture programme to reread the ten-year-old bestseller written by tonight's star guest, a well-known specialist in something or other. She will (at best) laugh in your face. All periods have their dominant illusions; no one is ever comfortably contemporary with the present. Our own time is characterized by the alliance of unprecedented means of information with unequalled impunity for the production of fakes: fake news, fake statistics, fake predictions. People have never *seen* so much of things, nor been so consistently wrong about their meaning. What we have gained in breadth of field we have lost in depth of time. A prayer to the powers that be: Give us less space, we humbly beg, and more time! Less live text and more follow-up!

Paid barkers and unschooled chroniclers are only doing their jobs when they announce and accredit idiocies: that has always been the case. The people I am talking about here are certified intelligences, moderate and eminent historians, creatures from the hushed inner circles of research and erudition. 'Soviet expansionism: central challenge of our time,' reads a headline in May 1981 – not on the front page of *France-Soir*, but on top of the leading article in our excellent review of ideas, *Le Débat*. 'There is no doubt', the piece begins, 'that future generations will be amazed by our blindness to the growth of Soviet power on the world stage.' A few pages further on, one of our most respectable philosophers, regarded as an authority by Sovietologists, concludes at the end of a meticulous analysis of the 'stratocracy' that the Soviet regime – his speciality –

> is suffering from a mild chronic illness from which it is incapable of recovering. It finds it impossible either to embark on reforms or to produce reformers. Even if an audacious and 'enlightened' new autocrat were to emerge at the top of the bureaucracy – an absurd hypothesis – he would not find a single group in the Party/State bureaucracy both willing and able to support him.

In a word, no prospect of 'major change'. The thing that deserves a moment's thought is not this nth proof of solid judgement – there are many other delectable examples in *Comment meurent les démocraties,** De la nature de l'URSS,*** La Force du vertige,*† and similar products of the intellectual *beau monde* – but the fact that the very same people who, for ten years, had filled the bookshops with utterly crazed works on the Eastern world could, in 1990, fill the

---

*(*Trans.*) Jean-François Revel.
**(*Trans.*) Edgar Morin.
†(*Trans.*) André Glucksman.

main lecture theatre at the Sorbonne with admirers at the invitation of our favourite magazine, the most intellectual of our weeklies; and, without batting an eyelid, start vaticinating on Gorbachev's future prospects.

Anyone who mentioned General de Gaulle in one of these innumerable seminars or 'special issues' (yesterday devoted to 'totalitarianism', today to 'whither the East?') would be treated as a risible halfwit. Minds are rigorously selective with information. The intellectual world sees nothing wrong with quoting and celebrating itself, but would find utterly ridiculous any reference to the trivialities of such a simple mind.

Is intelligence a plague? No, just a serious handicap. It has nothing to do with clairvoyance, despite the widespread delusion to that effect. In 1990, some of the best brains in France were predicting the non-violent advent, 'based on the sanctity of the social contract', of the 'United States of Europe', drawing a parallel with America in 1776 whose ineptness would be obvious to a seven-year-old child. Someone else announced: 'The main problem on the agenda is the extension of Democracy to the rest of the world', with the same unshaken aplomb that, twenty years earlier, accompanied the announcement of the preceding agenda, 'the extension of the Revolution to the rest of the world'. The most generous minds have been defending, in the name of morality, the moral monstrosity of the 'duty to intervene' (something that boils down to the right of the strong to invade Panama and do business with China). One is tempted to say, like a uniformed Groucho Marx staring in perplexity at a military map: 'Bring me a seven-year-old child.' Bring me General de Gaulle.

In the end the stuff of history is pretty crass – too crass, perhaps, for creatures of intellect like ourselves. It is rather embittering – let's admit it – after reading all the books and mortifying so much flesh,* to find that a profound reflection of the order 'Fécamp is a sea-port and intends to remain so'** contains such a clear 'effect

---

*(*Trans.*) Mallarmé: 'La chair est triste et lasse, et j'ai lu tous les livres . . .'
**(*Trans.*) De Gaulle, scraping the bottom of the barrel during a brisk visit to Fécamp.

of intelligence'. For example, it renders intelligible a more or less opaque tangle of strategies by making it possible finally to discern Russia as a continental country intending to become one again; Germany in the middle of Europe intending to reconstitute Mittel Europa; America, the world's big island, intending to remain so. It does not seem likely that geopolitics is all that underlies history. That would be too simple. All the same, to begin to see things clearly, it is a good idea to look at an atlas. 'So consult a map of the world,' Colonel de Gaulle used to urge his officers when they wilted over their operational maps.

I will venture a hypothesis to explain the mystery of the repeating error that so often afflicts those who are lawfully wedded to truth. What curse could have driven such respected persons as François Furet to be a Stalinist in 1950, as Debray to be a Castroite in 1960, as Glucksman to be a Maoist in 1970? Was it the same one that, some time later, drove them (except the second, enlightened in the interim by Guarani Indians and a few miraculous punches in the teeth) to become the same thing the other way round? I would identify this evil eye as an error of syntax, a solecism which cuts right across all vocabularies, red or white. We were simply wrong about the *subject*, the subject of history and of discourses on history. The places of subject, verb and object have been switched around. We made subjects – living entities, motive forces, active principles of development – out of things like Revolution and Democracy, with capital letters, which really are just predicate material. A phantasmagoria is an adjective used as a noun. A lot of countries have had a bourgeois economy and a working class. But the Bourgeoisie was no more a collective subject than the World Proletariat. Yes, there are democratic societies, as there are revolutionary situations. But democracy is not a social subject and revolution not an agent of history, to be embodied successively in this or that society or situation. There is something that existed before the 'democracy' condition, before the 'revolution' condition, and will survive them. Something older, more active, more durable, that for some time has been known by the vague name of 'nation'. It is relatively easy to distinguish a democracy from its counterfeit imitations; there are rules and criteria for the purpose. Defining a collective personality, distinguishing a nation from a

61

tribe or some other type of collectivity, is not so straightforward. But it is not because the idea of nation is badly defined that the reality it designates is not a determining one. Only idealists model reality on an idea of reality, and cut things down to match their representations.

Taking a pure idea for a motive force is a time-honoured speculative ailment which gives its victims a tremendous air of superiority. They, at least, know what they are talking about. Their minds are not cluttered with historical details, geographical accidents, cultural data. They go straight upstream to the root, to the heart of things; they unify the field, they globalize freehand. When he sees pears, strawberries and greengages before him, an imbecile will take care not to pile them together or put them all in the same bag. But an intelligent person plucks empirical fruit, utterly stupid fruit, the clear and easily definable idea of fruit (hard luck oh tomatoes); then sets out to demonstrate how the process of fructification will give rise to greengages, strawberries and pears through 'self-development' and 'self-institution' in the orchards of humanity. Replace the idea of Hegelian fruit with the idea of Revolution, then replace that with the idea of Democracy, and you will understand how easily, by means of a real effect of historical contagion across a fifty-year gap, illusions about the Democratic International come to replace those of yesterday's proletarian internationalism in our best minds. These illusions have the aggressive dynamic of Manichaeism. Fruit versus vegetable. Communism versus Bourgeoisie. Democracy versus Totalitarianism. Cosmopolitanism versus Nationalism. The fetishes come in pairs, handcuffed together by hatred. Devotees of the abstract are men who are 'against'. De Gaulle was a man *for.* He was no more anti-German than anti-Soviet, no more anti-American than anti-British. In fact he was all of these things, but only 'as required', by accident, not in his essence. His concept of the nation was not Manichaean; he paid no attention to the 'anti-Frenchness' so important to nationalists. There was nothing bipolar about his vision of the world.

Time is short. We need to find without a moment's delay people who are stupid, who know a bit about horticulture and can tell the difference between Romanian and Polish, Turkish and Albanian,

French and American. Did not a brainy socialist tell us recently that the real choice in France would henceforth be between adherents of the 'retrograde concept of national identity' and those of the 'democratic model of development'? Yet another single combat. Do we really have to choose between the concept of Fruit and the greengage? Between the idea of Democracy and the identity of our Republic, which is the concrete form Democracy has taken at the present stage of our cultural history? We are right to aspire to taste the finest products of nature, and to think about them together. But one at a time, in order of appearance: greengage first, concept second. De Gaulle on the subject of his lost referendum: 'What else could we do, these days? We had to choose democracy, so we had to have popular support.' This relativization of democracy resembles a scandalous shrug of the shoulders, on the scale of the epoch we are saddled with. *Sub specie historiae* it is rigorously logical: the French people had governments *before* the storming of the Bastille. It will probably still have them *after* what we now understand by democracy, perhaps after the storming of the Fraternity arch at la Défense, in a couple of hundred years' time.

At the heart of every historic gamble lies a decision on what is and is not useful to define as real. A separation of the absurd from the serious stuff. De Gaulle opted for the spirit of peoples; we chose legal convention and programmes based on *isms*. He won his bet; we have lost ours. Perhaps we had more brains, for what they were worth. But although there was less heavyweight text in his luggage, he had 'heroic judgement' which, according to Cardinal de Retz, consists in 'distinguishing between the extraordinary and the impossible'. In what it is usual to call 'macro-politics', de Gaulle forecast the most poetic event of our time, 'Europe from the Atlantic to the Urals', by putting the accent in exactly the right place in the prose of the period.

Visionary? No, down to earth. De Gaulle was no medium. It was we who were the Illuminati. He would look at something, make his diagnosis, and state his conclusion. 'It is a fairly common error', François Mitterrand writes, 'to see a visionary in this pragmatist, whose real genius lies in his eye for the immediate.' Absolutely. But we should beware of the convention that the artist is supposed to be unschooled, and genius purely spontaneous. You have to learn to be 'stupid'. It is not something that comes at the first attempt. De Gaulle never improvised. He trusted his instinct and did not talk gibberish. But he was guided by a prudent theory of instinct. 'Bergson', he said, 'has made me understand the philosophy of action. Action comes from the combination of intelligence and instinct. My whole life has been inspired by this. Pure intelligence cannot produce action by itself, while instinct can lead to folly if it is relied upon as a guide.' People think intuitively in the words of their time, using frames and categories established in their youth. The author of *Rire* was the most visible thinker of the turn of the century in France, just as the author of *L'Aiglon* was its great dramaturgist. The first of these left more of a mark on our young hobbledehoy, and it is to him that he owes his leitmotiv: the opposition between the mechanical and the living, between the artefact and the continuous, which throughout his life structured his action, his predictions, even his tirades ('The UN, that *gadget* ...'). The philosophy that supported this intuitive, empirical man – although he did not profess it – borrowed heavily from that very astute critique of intellectualism known as Bergsonism. (Its exile at the hands of post-1945 leading lights was not a positive development. Which of the two has worn better, Bergson or Heidegger?) A complicated mind and a convoluted language do not make a 'philosopher', as if the consistency of a thought had to be proportionate to its weight. De Gaulle had few ideas, none of them original. But it is a mistake to conclude that as a result, he did not integrate his political action with a concise and exact theory of the period. If that had been true, he would never have emerged from the barracks. The author of *La Discorde chez l'ennemi* knew that 'in war, apart from a few essential principles, there is no universal system, only circumstances and personalities'. But the author of *Mémoires de guerre* had learned that that was not enough to set a country back on its feet, and that it took more than character to understand in June 1940 that Hitler had lost the war. There is no Gaullist doctrine, but there is a Gaullian philosophy of history – more than a conviction, less than a system – which rationally disqualifies ratiocination while providing a sure and solid guide for improvisation. How much longer are we going to confuse the love of thought with the love of general ideas, when intellectual work consists precisely of producing concrete, singular ideas which cannot be generalized? How long are we going to believe that only philosophers can produce philosophy, on the pretext that the version put out by men of action has not been properly approved? Improvised philosophies, like occasional poems, are sometimes the finest of all. 'It's a funny thing, Bozel, destiny, don't you know? At the beginning of my life I believed I would be a soldier, and prepared myself for it. But I have not been a man of war. And you see me today a statesman. Now I am wondering whether my true destiny might not be as a philosopher, for I know that I have things to say to my contemporaries.'*

There is great art in welcoming the unforeseen, dominating chance events. And, for this purpose, discerning the underlying lines of force, whose nature does not change with regimes or generations of technology. For nothing is repeated in history, but nothing is ever really new. The underpinnings have an *indestructible* quality, a toughness, an enduring tenacity that is not to be found in the newspapers. Where they can be found is in Julius Caesar, Tacitus, Machiavelli, Shakespeare, Cardinal de Retz, Michelet, and so on. De Gaulle is not a seer but a reader. A rationalist. Not like Maurras;** like Auguste Comte. 'Know so as to foresee in order to act.' Know what? The *sub-jectum*. For what is underneath, and does not show through, will predominate in the long term. This is something that works. It enabled de Gaulle to be carried to power by partisans of French Algeria without once, even in 1958, telling them that Algeria was part of France. It enabled him to warn his contemporaries, prewar, that the diplomatic and military edifice of the Third Republic was going to collapse; postwar, that the institutional edifice of the Fourth was crumbling (and to predict in passing to Eisenhower, in Paris in 1956, that he would soon be back in power); then, under the Fifth, that the international monetary system was going to collapse as well. This necessarily

---

*Remarks made at Marly in January 1946.

**(*Trans.*) Charles Maurras (1868–1952), writer and opponent of political and artistic 'disorder'. Imprisoned in 1945 for collaboration.

caused him a fair amount of grief along the way. For his contemporaries, trusting by nature, resolutely optimistic, thought him a pain in the arse and jeered at him openly. That is what happens to people like him. Look back at the leading newspapers, consult the great minds of the period: Saint-John Perse at the quai d'Orsay, Mendès France at Matignon, Antoine Pinay;* none of them exactly an idiot.

'Catastrophes', Victor Hugo remarked, 'have a sombre way of sorting things out.' They certainly sorted out de Gaulle's affairs. It has often been said that historic figures are married to disgrace. But they do beget children on it. They are obliging Cassandras. De Gaulle was a prophet of doom, but one who thought ahead and proposed a solution to every misfortune. He compensated for catastrophe with willpower. The hardest thing in politics, the thing that distinguishes the statesman from the politician, is to want the consequences of what you want. These can be terrible. 1940 speaks for itself. It was meritorious to discern in 1959 that inter-continental missiles had rendered American military guarantees unfulfillable and NATO an anachronistic contraption (there are able men who have still to take this in, more than thirty years later). To deduce from this that in practice France could only really count on its own nuclear defences, and to invent a strategy for the weak facing the strong, was heroic. It was even optimistic and progressive – so much so that the Left at the time thought him insane. Someone who has grasped the *sub-jectum* often has good news to impart. In Warsaw, in 1967, de Gaulle announced its impending renaissance to the Polish nation; not long before, he had predicted the reunification of Germany to the Germans. To distinguish the artificial from the natural, or the ephemeral from the enduring, means outrunning the hare of the media astride the tortoise of old history books. It is something that gives a good laugh to devotees of the ephemeral, and it infuriates acolytes of the great machines. During the visit, in 1966, by 'the same France as always to the same Russia as always', de Gaulle replied when

---

*(*Trans.*) Independent deputy; former minister.

Soviet leaders asked him to recognize the GDR: Artificial creation. Won't last. Prussia, living entity. Will last. How we mocked him, in France, for calling Eastern countries by obsolete names, as if he was blind to the irreversible totalitarian upheaval! The old boy just could not grasp the fact that Communism had altered the European set-up. He went on stubbornly talking about 'Russia' as if we were still in the time of the Czars. Well, yes: 'Soviet Union', artefact, interesting but transitory, superficial. Won't last. 'Russia', serious entity, leathery, great people. Will endure. We need not mention Quebec, another hard nut destined for a long life. It is not lunatic to bet on the self-determination of peoples, those irrepressible *sub-jecta*. But it is fanciful to attempt *to make a mobilizing project out of a phoney subject*: the European Community, for example, which is being 'constructed' behind the backs of the peoples, between the lines of real life. A likeable but artificial creation which (alas!) won't last. The problem is that the legislator of the future should have been seen in his lifetime as a 'frozen mammoth', an albatross, an elderly bull in a china shop, while the mechanical model maker, the Meccano enthusiast, passes for a great humanist. Although in this world the loser often takes all, the politician always opts to win at once, even if it means losing later. It was not sound politics to say in 1969 that the French Senate is not particularly useful (true) and that the time had come to establish regional administrations (premature). An adroit politician would have dropped that inept referendum. The coming together of a lucidity and a popularity, of a historic figure and the interplay of parties, smacks of the miraculous (if that is the right word for a national or world catastrophe that suspends the parliamentary game, sidelines the professionals, and gives the talented amateur his chance). 1940, 1958: world war, civil war, texts and traditions inapplicable. Pushed to centre stage by these two bouts of near-illicit horseplay, the marginal figure each time found his path unblocked, until the pretence-system blown away by the crisis managed to reconstitute itself and stop him, sending him – a prophet in his own country – back to his primary solitude. May 1968, a catastrophe prevented, was not quite disastrous enough to cause another ferment or establish new public holidays.

Let's speak clearly: de Gaulle saw and predicted what the Left neither saw nor predicted. In 1963 the Left condemned the veto on British entry to the Common Market, in the name of the political Europe Britain has been obstructing ever since. It opposed the French nuclear deterrent; in 1964 it urged the signing of the non-proliferation treaty, in the name of the world peace which nuclear deterrence had at last made possible. It criticized the decision to leave NATO on the grounds that it might offend our oldest ally, which ten years later congratulated itself, and France, on an astute move. It jeered at the Phnom Penh speech in which de Gaulle told America that it had lost the Vietnam War, and advised an honourable settlement through political negotiation, on the grounds that France should not meddle in what does not concern it. In 1967 it accused him of being anti-Semitic, quoting out of context the reference to an 'elite people, sure of itself and domineering' (a compliment in his terms, as Ben-Gurion himself acknowledged soon afterwards) in his solitary (and rigorously accurate) warning that 'occupation of the territories conquered by Israel cannot proceed without oppression, repression and expulsions, and without the occupants meeting resistance, which they will describe as terrorism'. Israeli democracy has now recognized that it cannot survive for long if occupation of these territories continues. The Left did not recognize the 'Palestinian problem' while it was being born, or notice the signs of impending disintegration in the Lebanon (something de Gaulle feared as early as 1968 when, for that very reason, he condemned the first Israeli raid on Beirut airport).

Of course the nature of reality has subsequently reconciled the French Left to a lot of things it did not understand at the time: nuclear deterrence, special status in the Atlantic alliance, Middle East policy, openness to Eastern Europe, and so on. Not forgetting the institutions conceived and established by 'Napoleon IV' the semi-presidential system on which the new Soviet democracy is explicitly modelled. It was in the Left's interests, this belated gratitude, and well merited, for it was de Gaulle who made France a present of Mitterrand. Everyone knows that without the right of dissolution, the notion of presidential majority and the election by universal suffrage of a President for seven years, the Left would have had to pack its bags soon after 1981. De Gaulle and the

Constitution established democracy in a monarchical country with a penchant for civil war. Yet we suspected for years that he was there to extirpate it.

When a 'reactionary' is always first aboard the train of the future, while a 'progressive' regularly turns up panting as it steams away, there is something amiss with our categories. Left/Right implies Change versus Immobilism; 'The Right follows history, the Left precedes it,' as Jacques Ruffié pithily wrote. So what do we call a Left which does not foresee or prepare for the future? Another Right, a pessimist would say. A Left which has finally learned not to go faster than the music, an optimist would reply. Even so, it helps to have some idea of the score, an important aid to dancing in step. When the tempo speeds up, the margin between someone who is ahead of 'the terrible rhythm of events' and someone hurrying to keep up can be measured in hours or days. This has been plain to see since the demolition of the Berlin Wall. For nearly a year now, our governments have invariably been a week behind events in Europe.

A man who predicts the worst in order to arrange things for the best is called a 'pessimist'. A man who lulls us to sleep by predicting the best, while allowing the worst to occur, is congratulated for being an 'optimist'. The 'aristocratizing pessimism' discerned in de Gaulle by Jean Daniel, the most Gaullist of our left-wingers, prevented quite a few misfortunes; the democratic optimism of Léon Blum failed to prevent a number of terrible ones (including destruction of the Spanish Republic and the rise of fascism). The perceived temperament of the Right seems to be more adapted to international confrontation, that of the Left to internal amelioration. Outside, so to speak, a state of nature prevails between sovereign entities, each country reserving the right (United Nations and great oaths notwithstanding, and irrespective of political regime) to make its own justice. The law of the jungle that prevails in international society can and should be *softened* but not *abolished*. In external action, pessimism implies vigilance, promptness, anticipation. Within a democracy, on the other hand, the primacy of law and the courts is not a meaningless idea. In the internal context, pessimism about human nature degenerates into conservatism. Every temperament has its field of ability.

International life is right-wing, like nature. The social contract is left-wing, like humanity. De Gaulle was a genius in foreign policy, but he had no more than a talent for domestic affairs. Will the opposite be said one day of Mitterrand? Let us hope so. The worst thing would be a Left which put its cynicism in the wrong place: which assented to an imbalance of forces internally, where laws and regulations could be applied, and put its faith in contractual law externally, where relations of force are all that matter. This would provide all the drawbacks of the Left without any of its advantages: neither social progress nor foreign policy, neither internal justice nor external capability.

*

We did not foresee the return of the ancient in brand-new condition, God in alliance with computers, the reappearance of Europe's former outlines. Those who thought they knew what was going on did not; the man everyone thought an outsider was in the thick of things. The dinosaur in a képi, the man whom Sartre – like today's modernists – saw as 'an old sorcerer whose function is to keep us in the dark at all costs', has come through the mirror to meet the 'new man' from the depths of the future, where all sorcery has disappeared.

Sartre and the others cannot really be blamed. De Gaulle combined all the handicaps: a bourgeois Catholic military chauvinist. Nothing more backward could be conceived.

Of course our braggart did display some interesting discrepancies, which were not lost on astute observers like Althusser, who used to nag in the rue d'Ulm: 'Father de Gaulle, all the same, well worth a closer look.' A nationalist whose first concern on coming to power was to reconcile us with the hereditary enemy; a Maurrassian who, in 1936, wanted France to fight for the Spanish Republic; an old military officer condemned to death in 1940 by a court martial; a reactionary who ignored the atavistic theme of decadence, and always substituted 'hope for what is to come' for 'regret for what has gone'; a king without a camarilla, a monarch without a court, whose transparent Household displayed more self-denial than ambition and did not encroach on government; a demagogue who was careful to keep the opinion media at arm's length; the author of the 'permanent *coup d'état*' who surrendered the state at the first electoral setback: in short, a character not calculated to make us smug about the stereotype. Be that as it may, though: he was still a man of the Right.

The shapes of towns and the meanings of words change more quickly, alas, than the heart of a mortal. The way the world is going, de Gaulle will be given the benefit of the doubt on that. Appointing a director of the Rothschild Bank to the post of Prime Minister seemed to us in 1961 the height of cynicism. A lot of socialists today would be more than happy to prove their seriousness in this way. How pusillanimous we thought the General's reformist leanings on the 'social question'! Yet any socialist minister, today, would go scarlet with annoyance at the mention of his leftist rubbish – ideas like 'participation' and 'capital–labour partnership'. Nobody even talks about 'capitalism' these days, or mentions 'capital' and 'labour'. Bourgeois? Of course he was. We have not seen all that many workers at the top of the state since his time, in the ministries or even in the local administrations. That grand-bourgeois paternalist certainly lacked fraternity, but he had a sense of equity. Petty-bourgeois careerists often have neither.

Proletarians did not go to Saint-Cyr, granted. But the aspirant officer, with or without a *de* to his name, is not just any bourgeois. People do not pursue military careers merely to secure a reserved seat when travelling by train. You can make fun of the uniform, but you cannot despise it. Unless you venerate money.

Anti-militarism is a Jacobin quality, and a pretty recent one at that. The Left's indifference to military matters, on the other hand, has done it a great deal of harm. It is conceded that military individuals may possess character, but historical intelligence is thought to remain our property. It is certainly true that the military institution has been on the wrong side at every crossroads of the century, from Dreyfus to Algeria. But it is within the armed forces that the most sagacious as well as the most courageous criticisms are made. It is also true that in France, political reflection is not often to be found in officer-training courses; but to conclude from this that nobody in the mess has a thought in his head is frivolous. Where do people read more, or better, than they do in training for the Navy? Which of the two, on average, will be the more cultivated: an undergraduate or a naval officer? Are General Poirier and General Buis,* to name but two, 'military' authors? Are Vauvenargues and Vigny just imbeciles? The time-honoured militant's reflex of contempt for Blimpishness – the idea that pips on the shoulder mean a severely limited outlook – betrays a certain misconception about thought itself, which in every epoch has included a crystalline nucleus of military strategy. 'Behind Alexander's victories, Aristotle is always to be found.... There is not a single illustrious Captain without a taste and a feeling for the heritage of the human mind' (de Gaulle). 'The real school of command', he added when teaching at the École de Guerre as a lieutenant-colonel, 'is general culture.' The general culture of the Left, on the other hand, pays very little attention to command problems, to the great joy of the military Staffs whose most backward elements find themselves in charge when the Left is in power. A proper anti-militarism presupposes a smattering of knowledge about the military environment, its techniques and technologies. Without it, the anti-militarist will become putty in the hands of the military-industrial establishment, whose margin of manoeuvre is at its widest under a government of vacuous civilians. Furthermore, the best way to give the secret services a free hand to commit, and cover up, all sorts of baroque illegal acts is to decline direct responsibility for them (in France, unlike the other great democracies, they were long ago abandoned to the armed forces). In short, it is idle to suppose that the comic trooper is always skiving. The author of *La Discorde chez l'ennemi*, who required the civil authority to live up to its responsibilities, did not allow the military to conduct the war, but only (at most) individual operations. This curious general, who did not hesitate to condemn a fellow general to death for plotting to kill him, had so little reverence for the institution that after making it swallow defeat in Algeria, he went on rubbing it up the wrong way by imposing strategic nuclear weapons (bugbear of the Army) and withdrawal

---

*(*Trans.*) Theoreticians of French nuclear deterrence in the 1960s, recognized as very intellectual officers.

from NATO (a body rich in military sinecures). On these matters our socialist leaders have been more accommodating. They rallied to NATO politically (just before it was shelved); in 1984, Reagan *imperatore*, they designated the USSR the official enemy (there was, of course, no time to lose); they espoused the joint disarmament negotiations at Vienna (shortly before the blocs disintegrated); and finally, despite a defence minister isolated by his own lucidity, they joined the demagogic chorus in support of disarmament (just as Europe was becoming dangerous again). The strategic choices confronting our defence architecture – as serious in their way as those France faced in the 1930s – are not made easier by trying to run with the hare and hunt with the hounds. The result is that the supreme reference of our armed forces remains the *Livre blanc** of 1972, now almost prehistoric.

Does electoral alternation force people into a game of wrong-footing the adversary, attempting to disarm him by playing his game better than he does himself? This may explain how a Left government came to fill all the posts under its patronage with representatives of the Right ... something the Right has never managed to pull off in times of victory. It does not seem to have grasped the principle of sound government: do what the adversary would never have dared attempt in the same place.

'But surely,' I hear someone saying, 'the clearest indication that this Déroulède** was entering the future backwards was that he placed the national question above the social question, when it was quite obvious that national divisions were disappearing. The national theme has always been the defining characteristic of the right (e.g. National Front). Obviously the nationalism of rejection suited this backward, resentful man. Stalin flattered him in 1944: hence the Franco–Soviet treaty and the suspect indulgence towards the Communist world. A little earlier he had been vexed by Roosevelt. Hence his unhealthy anti-Americanism, his

---

*(*Trans.*) A government text equivalent to a British White Paper.
**(*Trans.*) Paul Déroulède (1846–1914), writer and politician, president of the League of Patriots, author of *Chants du soldat.*

vengeance on his successors. "I, General de Gaulle, me . . .". Hardly surprising that the Cassandra of national egotism should have had such a boundless ego.'

This sort of drivel points to our blind spot, the nucleus of the misunderstanding.

8

The nation or the great

misunderstanding

Nationalism is a hideous evil which, since its appearance just two centuries ago, has disfigured mankind and the planet. De Gaulle's version of the nation was not a continuation of this pox by other means, but the beginning of a cure.

It is impossible to exaggerate the fatal ambiguity of this word *nation*, which confuses two hostile sisters. Ethnic communion and elective community; race and people; Right and Left. The Germanic forest and the Bill of Rights. What Stefan Zweig (in *Souvenirs d'un Européen*) called the 'nationalist pestilence' is derived from the first meaning; *Long live all nations,* which is what the soldiers at Valmy really meant when they shouted *Long live the nation* – opening, in Goethe's words, a new era in the history of humanity – derives from the second. Those who attack nationalism at random are like experts on the Dreyfus Affair who use the same word to describe the pro-Dreyfus and anti-Dreyfus camps. Hardly the best way to clarify things.

De Gaulle was a pro-Dreyfus officer who disowned his caste without discarding the uniform. 'It's crazy!' exclaimed the 'Constable's'* mother one day, 'My sons are republicans.' And Charles was a steadfast believer in Dreyfus's innocence.

He never talked in terms of 'roots', 'purity', 'foreign bodies' or

---

*(*Trans.*) 'Le Connétable', one of de Gaulle's nicknames, means Constable in the medieval sense of a king's steward or administrator.

'contamination'. The term 'national *identity*' was foreign to him. So, in another direction, was the humanitarian pacifism of Zola and his successors. The France he envisaged was the opposite of 'France for the French'.

He always avoided *defining* his nation, or even (like Stalin) the nation in general. He produced images of it, subjective impressions, without (like Maurras) assembling them into a specific formula; in this he preferred poetic to philosophic wisdom. It is a reassuring sign. To isolate the substance of a nation is to define the nation as a substance. Let us call a 'nationalist' a person who believes that his country's essence precedes its existence. De Gaulle was one of those for whom existence precedes essence. This is a definition in itself: the definition of a patriot, one who does not – like a Maurrassian – make a fetish of his country, endowing it with a divine primacy over all others. De Gaulle was an existentialist of the nation, and of governmental legitimacy. So far as he was concerned the act does not establish the right, merely precedes it; as, in his view, the call of 18 June – a necessary contingency – marked the irrevocable origin of his legitimacy.

*

I abhor 'nationals', but I do not include de Gaulle.

Because I regard as inventive – albeit not impeccable – a conception of the nation which brings law into the forests. By challenging both romantic organicism (the nation as a fusional organism, devouring the rights of the individual) and juridical artificiality (the nation as a social contract and civil agreement between individuals). The latter, to keep things short, dates from the French eighteenth century; the former from the German nineteenth. With a bow in the direction of dialectic, it might be said that de Gaulle embodied a third moment, beyond the Teutonic Vaterland and the American political convention: the nation as *symbolic heritage*, beyond the primitive tribe but on this side of the 'body of associated persons living under a common law' (Sieyès). His nation is an act not of nature but of culture, located at the confluence of a history and a purpose. Of a mother tongue which is not chosen, and a legislation which is discussed and voted in common. Something lighter than 'the earth and the dead'* but more substantial than a parchment or an oath. He opposed the barbaric language of the hereditary and racial 'community' with the idea of the *assembly*: a free, individual act.

A 'nation' which nobody can possess, as if it were a simple collective, but which is not imposed on us in the form of a duty to commune, is not the mask of a ruthless will to power. It cannot turn 'the right of peoples to decide their own future' – a negative right, to resist oppression – into a right to trample on neighbours; because such a nation does not award itself any ontological superiority over others. It expresses a desire for liberty, not domination. German Romanticism supplied pan-Germanism with legitimacy, of a sort; de Gaulle did not attempt to confront it with pan-Gallicism. The nation in French form, heritage of '89 and '93, is neither an end in itself nor a supreme value; it is the first stage of the universal, turning the patriot towards humanity as a whole instead of shutting him into his circumscribed animal's territory. De Gaulle was not of the Jacobin clan, but a Jacobin can live with propositions like: 'France should serve the universal values of humanity', or: 'The only cause that counts is that of mankind'. Hardly the words of a chauvinist.

Yes, we have been lucky: Barrès, in the world of yesterday, met Michelet; Richelieu met Montesquieu. 'The genius is the man who reconciles the most opposites' (Hegel). This genius, in 1940, got the warrior Leclerc and the jurist Cassin to shake hands. Nationalism in its raw form usually generates a demagogic authoritarian populism. De Gaulle was a cool, measured patriot who tempered the warmth of collective Romanticism with a very classical, almost icy sense of the state ruled by law; restrained the emotional lyricism of the specific with the austerity of the general rule. This alleged megalomaniac was repelled by Wagnerian extremes of France-worship, by anything excessive or baroque. For the Nietzschean – and Christian – de Gaulle, 'the divine game of the hero' ends where the Decalogue begins. His sense of measure and

---

*(*Trans.*) 'La terre et les morts', an old lugubrious slogan of French nationalism.

balance in internal affairs gave him a sense of the *possible* in external policy: a precise awareness of how far he could go. 'There has only *been* a France by virtue of the state,' he often said. The bony armature supporting the flesh of the nation: no 'assembled nation' without a 'sound state' and 'up-to-date defences'. And the Bard of Gaul was first and foremost Head of State; a state ready for emergencies – see Article 16 of the Constitution – but in normal times subject to the republican rule of suffrage, popular repre- sentation and arbitration. The nation is the source of all power, which can be exercised only in its name; the nation is the sole founder of public authority which nobody – individual, party, ideology or class – can appropriate. 'The Republic', he used to say, 'is not palaces, or ushers, or telephones. The Republic is the people.'

The nation-state makes the sovereign-citizen: Tartempion hires and fires the big cheese. The synonymy of citizen and patriot was a singular product of the French Revolution. The mystique of '93 fuses, like Hugo, 'great wars between fatherlands, the colossal fall of tyrants'. It could be that there was some 'incompatibility of humour between General de Gaulle and democracy' (Mitterrand, 1965). He was certainly too inclined to reduce trust to a matter of allegiance, universal suffrage being there solely to endorse the chief. Nevertheless, it seems to me that in spirit, if not always to the letter, and despite his anti-parliamentarism and unhealthy taste for 'clear and massive Yes votes', de Gaulle kept faith with the revolutionary pact, unique in Europe, sealed in 1789 between the two religions of liberty and the nation.

Chauvinism is to independence as Communism is to equality and sickness to health. Do you give up your hold on life just because you are ill? Those who invoke the evil nationalist tempta- tion to get at de Gaulle through Le Pen, as others use Pol Pot to liquidate Jaurès, are committing a bad act. As if the choice in 1940 had been between internationalism and nationalism ... and not between de Gaulle and Pétain, or two incompatible perceptions of national existence. Suppose the dilemma of the year 2000, in Europe and elsewhere, turned out not to be 'federalism versus nationalism' but de Gaulle's nation versus Le Pen's tribe?

Clichés are deadly, tags kill. De Gaulle goes down before

them every day. Read in your newspaper about the unbreakable antithesis between 'jingoist decline' and 'the European adventure'; the defenders of identity and supporters of adaptation; believers in exclusion and believers in openness; men of memories and men of projects. In short, between old and young, dodgy old geezers in berets and wideawake dynamic self-starters. In this journalistic phantasmagoria – Modernity versus Archaism, Europeans versus Jacobins, and so on – de Gaulle, of course, symbolizes the negative pole. Everyone knows that he left his successors a backward France, without scientific research or new technologies, without rockets or aircraft, without a nuclear industry, without motorways or computers . . .

Our conditioned reflexes are strong enough to maintain the historical hallucination. It is in good faith that our stereotypes falsify texts, annul the facts; open the trapdoor under the greatest modernizer of contemporary France and drop him out of sight. Null and void, the 1961 and 1962 proposals for a union of European States, 'a Europe existing by itself and for itself'. You would think de Gaulle had barricaded himself in his castle, that he had not proposed in 1964, to the Community States in Strasbourg, that they 'realize and apply between them in the political field, which is primarily the defence field, an organization which would of course be allied with the New World, but which would be their own in terms of its objectives, means and commitments'. Pretty funny feudal castle, whose lord entrusted all-round defence to squadrons of Mirage IVs, soon supplemented by submarines invisibly wandering the oceans. The view that the nation-state is a historically obsolete category, squeezed between the infranational order of regions and constituencies and the supranational order of European institutions and multinational companies, and that it is appropriate to speed up its death throes, has every appearance of realism (and that alone is plenty). But it is hardly an excuse for confusing de Gaulle with Pétain, the apostle of mechanized manoeuvres with the supporter of defensive earthworks. It does not justify associating a domanial and patrimonial France, a France of bigwigs and miserly peasants, focal point and paddock, exclusive, preventive, strung about with genealogies and excommunications, a France people do not carry away on the soles of their shoes,* with the man who embodied in his lifetime 'the very provisional victory of a peripheral France, a changing France in search of new worlds and new knowledge, over the deeply rooted France of withdrawal and introversion' (Jean Lacouture).

*

The national fact is not a fact but an idea. It has the air of a self-evident truth, but it is an enigma. It is also a troubled feeling, a suspect passion ... all those words pregnant with facile emotion. Strong feeling, attended by weak definition. Instead of looking for the reason in this unreason, we continue to set Reason and its defenders (us) against the Nation and its loonies (them). It is so much more comfortable that way.

The national Sphinx talks like Monsieur de Lapalisse** ('France, because she is France ...'), but in action it kills: its devotees, but more especially its denigrators, those who disdain to respond to it.

For two centuries, all the major defeats suffered by the Left throughout the world have resulted from its refusal to pay attention to what it amusingly calls the 'national question'. By the same token, it owes its victories to its marriages with this unreal reality.

For a century, this refusal had a title (Marxism) and a social reason (the Workers' International). Today it is called modernity, and hides behind the undeniably worldwide scale of production and exchange. But there is no reason to suppose that failure to recognize the national fact will be less costly tomorrow than it was yesterday.

The nation just now is in the situation of sexuality before Freud. It is not thought nice to go too deeply into that kernel of obscurity, that shameful crypt of the Enlightenment. We on the Left are the Victorians of the nation, strangled by prudery. The systematic

---

*(*Trans.*) Celebrated phrase of Danton's.
**(*Trans.*) 1470–1525; Marshal of France. Soldier and statesman, renowned for simplicity. Lampooned in a poem by Bernard de la Morroye; hence a byword for stating the self-evident.

neglect of the 'maleficent genius' de Gaulle, and his belittlement by current sociological models, originate in a moral (if not especially honourable) response to the excesses and ignominies of nationalism. Sexuality, too, is responsible for innumerable crimes, follies and perversions. That is why psychology used to follow common sense in making it a taboo, and why the first person to recognize the polymorphous perversity seething in our dear little blond heads was able, soon afterwards, to witness his books being burned. Obviously the fellow was an obsessive, libidinous in private and pan-sexualist in theory. In the same way, anyone who lends an ear to the national unconscious soon finds himself taxed with nationalism. Sade and Freud, each in his own way, brought the Enlightenment into the bedroom. Who will bring it into the fatherlands and mother countries? In practice the 'talking cure' does not aim to rouse sleeping wolves but to domesticate them by bringing them out of the shadows. It is not so much sexuality as its denial that makes perversion; and denial of the national fact has done a thousand times more damage in the world than its recognition. Europeans should assume that the nations exist, and learn to live with them. Otherwise, watch out: what they have repressed will come back and seize them by the throat.

The nationality principle, they say, carried within it the seeds of the 1914 War ... unless it was the imperial principle that stirred the nationalities up by crushing them. The partitioning of nations under the Versailles Treaty engendered, they say, the Second World War. Unless the dismantling of Austria-Hungary and the Ottoman Empire by the victors at Versailles led to the formation of fake nation-states, without historical reality...

The nation is not the answer to all the challenges of our time, for it is a problem in itself. Indeed, it is *the* problem: once you have got hold of the wire, you can pull as hard as you like without breaking it.

A people, he used to say, 'like the olive tree, never dies'. There is always an epistemological risk in comparing a level of reality we do not yet know with an earlier level we know better. De Gaulle is not a history of science professor. To approach this mysterious living entity which persists and signals its presence over time, to pin down the subject–object which is a collective individual, he proceeds by metaphor, by analogy. What is a national spirit? The way he talks about it places him closer to biology than to geometry or mechanics, closer to instinct than to intelligence. It has little to do with measurement or matter, but is close to memory in the Bergsonian sense: not a faculty for classifying or registering things remembered, but a sort of germinative retentiveness, a past–present, a thrust of creative evolution occurring after plants, animals and individual awareness.

Gaullian France, in any case, is not a thing to be measured and counted. That France is Pétain's. Secure in the support of the inhabitants, the regions, the real institutions, the Marshal drew his legitimacy from the soil and the sociology. It was the France favoured by Roosevelt, who liked to have a solid interlocutor with access to the cash-drawer, and was not too keen on this landless Charles-figure who heard voices like Joan of Arc and claimed, for four long years, a legitimacy without tangible backing. It is true that a concept of legitimacy which is not based exclusively on popular representation endangers democracy. 'The letter kills and the spirit vivifies.' But a spirit without a letter quickly becomes a deed of Prince or Prophet. De Gaulle in 1940 placed the spirit of the Republic above its letter until such time as they could be reunited. Had he not taken this terrible risk in June 1940, Pétain – legally invested under regular constitutional procedure by a freely elected Chamber – would have remained the sole holder of national legitimacy, for he really was France according to the letter. Many valiant soldiers stayed loyal to Pétain out of respect for the given word: an armistice had been legally signed with the occupant, and a country cannot break a signed treaty without dishonour. Juridically it was impeccable. From this point of view, the 'terrorists' were rebels without honour wanted by the law – something Jean Paulhan* rightly recalled to the 'directors of the Resistance' at the time of the purge. But they had chosen France according to the spirit.

Gaullian France is an absence. An idea, an 'invincible dream'.

---

*(*Trans.*) 1884–1968. Writer and critic; director of the influential *Nouvelle revue française*.

An image rather, a Madonna or fairy-tale princess. Not a photo-image, a painting. Of the vanished, absent Mother, gone to dinner in town leaving her child behind. The boy closes his eyes: and there she is. France not as a land but a firefly: only really visible in the dark, from a distance. Counting and listing would spoil it. Pétain's is an exact reproduction of the state of things (and minds) in the Hexagon of 1940: Kodak click-clack. De Gaulle's paintbrush describes a sovereign dynamic of imagination, an internal and wholly immaterial France, in the setting of the outside world. He does this in a way that is pragmatic, not incantatory. In the beginning was the fable, every nation starts from a fabulation. France is an effect of language, born out of a tangle of narratives; de Gaulle, a voluntarist of the imagination.

Was he an early futurist of nationality? He saw France as a 'raw immaterial', and the national being has since (as do all things) dematerialized. It has taken off, departed from its physical moorings. The Hexagon defended from space, from the depths of the oceans, is *res nullius*. So the man who saw his country not as a territory but as a vocation, not a place but a call, may have announced (as 'steward of the spirit of the universe') the current process of transition from substance-country to radiance-country, from dead memory (repetitive, with a fixed schedule) to living memory (on which new data can be inscribed); from nation-as-storehouse to nation-as-message. From localization to ubiquity. Or, if you prefer, from Péguy–Déroulède to Deleuze–Guattari.

*

There were, are and always will be two Frances. An earthbound continental France with Finistère guarding its back and its ramparts facing east, which regards the sea as simply the end of the land and squints mistrustfully at anything overseas; and a France of broad horizons – the sea does not lie* – open to the far reaches, welcoming to offshore cultures, relying on trade and its Navy; a France that needs the whole world precisely because it thinks of

---

*(*Trans.*) Echoing Pétain: 'La terre ne ment pas.'

itself as a big mythical island like Britain or Japan, but more curious than the others because it is more sure of itself. (A country's capacity for solitude often goes in tandem with its capacity for openness: France has never shone more brightly in the outside world than during the 'isolation' of the de Gaulle years.)

The first plays the game of weakness confronting strength: sea-to-land or air-to-surface. The second plays a game of strength versus strength: surface-to-surface.

It takes a little of everything to make the history of a people. Amphibious France, with its two geographies, can certainly allow itself two strategies: one peasant and one maritime. A European strategy and a world strategy – never equally balanced, but alternating.

De Gaulle, an army man, was forced in 1940 to play France's hand from the sea, and he made a virtue of this necessity until the end; Mitterrand's France has always had both feet planted on the ground. The first saw Europe against a planetary background. The second sees the planet against a European background.

*

Myth is in charge, myth and the individual. Something said by Mackinder* can also be said in the manner of La Bruyère. For a strategy is the expression of a character. The soul of de Gaulle's France is an unending interior quest; that of Mitterrand's France is a physical certitude, a field of wheat in the sunshine. 'I do not need an idea of France,' Mitterrand once said. 'I can see France. I have an instinctive, profound awareness of France, France as a physical entity.... A people that clings to the land becomes inseparable from it.' And on another occasion: 'I love France in my own fashion, which is that of a peasant gazing over his land in spring: someone who weighs the price of things, who knows what his precious wheat has cost in patience and sacrifice.'

One is a prophet haunted by history, the other an observer given to geographical delectation ('I have a passion for her

---

*(*Trans.*) Harold Mackinder, a turn-of-the-century geographer, strategist and military theorist.

geography, her living body'). Two strong souls deriving their strength from opposite sources. Audacity against subtlety. Eagerness versus tenacity. The storm-lashed island of Sein against peaceful inland Charente ('I was born in Saintonge, in half-tone France ...'*).One needed tempests, crises, thunder and lightning; the other is content with the rhythm of the passing days: 'a sun that rises and sets, the sky overhead, the scent of wheat, the odour of dogs, the sequence of the hours'. Put it any way you like: *le Bateau ivre* or 'life there is peaceful and straightforward'. Claudel or Chardonne. Stormy weather or the passage of the seasons.

One took the weather in his face, the wind in his teeth. The other adopts an oblique approach, and hopes to avoid getting wet. There are men who break through and men who manoeuvre. The tactic of affront and the tactic of camouflage. There is an art in dramatizing things; and another in dedramatizing them. Two temperaments, two styles, two versions of France. 'Sometimes fox, sometimes lion,' Machiavelli said, advising the Prince to be both. But people are what they are.

In emergencies de Gaulle was pre-emptive; Mitterrand is reactive. The lion provokes a clash and actively seeks crisis; the fox equivocates and tries to gain time. The soldier sharpens angles; the civilian smooths them out. Some people get rough; others jink and dodge.

Or, to put it more respectably, the imprudent soldier made scenes, the foxy civilian never puts a foot wrong.

Flaubert once admitted that 'you have to hallucinate a bit to make literature'. How many stories do you have to tell yourself in order to make a bit of history?

'There is no need for me to be told stories about France. My feelings about her can do without eloquence.' And Mitterrand adds: 'If I had been a writer, I would not have been an imaginative one.' Nor are Jules Renard, Fromentin, Zola and Chardonne, the writers of his 'family'.

The trouble comes when the wind rises outside, when real

---

*(*Trans.*) Mitterrand.

history starts showing enough imagination for anyone. Then the realist may be left on the starting line by *objective craziness*, and go quietly crazy in the hollow of his peasant sagacity.

Both of these republican monarchs were taught by Jesuits. But St Ignatius of Loyola can be understood in two ways: intransigence, to save the soul; and cunning, to save the furniture. Mitterrand accused de Gaulle of 'confusing love of country with the insolence of national pride'. I cannot help wondering whether de Gaulle would have accused Mitterrand of confusing adjustment to the terrain with compromises with heaven.

It is true that every quality has its caricature, and that it is possible to justify 'arrogance' by referring to 'cunning', and vice versa, in a sort of virtuous circle.

The lesser of these two extremes is the one to choose, and this is done by circumstances, depending on the balance of force. A weak or defeated country should be inflexible; a country that is strong or in a solid position can afford to be pleasant.

'Do as I do, General,' Churchill urged in 1942, 'I bend before Roosevelt, then stand up again.'

'I'm too poor, I couldn't,' de Gaulle replied.

This is a constant of meteorological strategy in our country. In ordinary times we are on terra firma and can give time to the weather. But when 'the hurricane of history' returns, we are not going to find a sheltered mooring by line-of-sight navigation. Then we have to be able to abandon the parish pump, forget about 'quiet strength'* and evasive answers, and head for the open sea.

---

*(*Trans.*) *La force tranquille*: Mitterrand electoral slogan.

9

Young and old

Mockingly or admiringly, many on the Left and elsewhere have echoed Mitterrand's judgement on the late de Gaulle: that he was 'the last of the nineteenth-century great men', along the lines of a Metternich or a Bismarck. Most of them are jeering at a backward promoter of national isolation, a big prat swathed in negative grandeur. François Mitterrand, of course, is not being ironic. He is simply acknowledging de Gaulle's greatness for what it is: that of a founding personality, 'in the style of the captains and war leaders of the nineteenth century'; on the ball when it comes to a war in the military field, a bit slow on the question of peace everywhere else.

It occurs to me that the course of things may have played one of its habitual low tricks on us. Consider the possibility that de Gaulle was really the first great man of the twenty-first century, and that it is Mitterrand who is the last one of the nineteenth. Perhaps we all saw the realist as an illusionist, and thought him anachronistic when really he was awkward for other reasons. Perhaps it is we who are the naive ones in this story: for failing to see that the one has presided over the final collapse of Papa's socialism – a fresher tradition, of course, than our grandparents' liberalism, but similarly rooted in 1848 – while the other prefigured the post-realism of the post-industrial era.

Just a thought. An impious one, granted, but somewhat less sterile than the pious certitudes we hear most of the time; so long as we can define what to accept as real in the hurly-burly of change.

Every reality has at least two faces: heads and tails.

Mitterrand once described de Gaulle's France as a mixture of Royer-Collard* and Richelieu. Princes of ambiguity always understand one another.

The Royer-Collard face, 'tails', makes de Gaulle seem terribly old. It evokes an old bourgeois patriarchal France, yes-Papa yes-boss yes-darling, churches full every Sunday, furtive sexuality, hidden money, hard collars, long skirts, ORTF as the 'voice of France', the state's hand in everything. Sociologically and economically dead and buried, this early postwar France is now mouldering in the Museum of Bourgeois Arts and Sciences. Feminism, Larzac,** free radio, *Actuel*, homosexuals, recognition of minorities, revival of the regions – the whole 1968 mutation – have swept it into the past, never to be seen again. Good riddance!

The Richelieu face, 'heads' – the important side, in my opinion – makes de Gaulle seem tremendously young. For temporary, conjunctural reasons and for permanent, fundamental ones.

The conjunctural reasons, to do with the change in the material and moral décor, are obvious to any European. Foreign policy has become so urgent and absorbing that it eclipses domestic politics; the old national question threatens – as usual when things get dramatic – to overshadow social issues. The whole of Europe is becoming Gaullian, willy-nilly. For the first time in thirty years, Europe is going to have to live with 'the prospect' of war (in the philosophic sense of the expression). Old-style strategists will be in work again (but not with tanks this time). There is no instance of an empire crumbling peacefully without setting off conflicts in its peripheral regions, and there is no reason to suppose that the Soviet Empire will be any better in this area than the Ottoman or Austro-Hungarian ones. Germany has taken only thirty years, the blink of an eye, to confirm de Gaulle's forecast made in 1959: 'The reunification of the two parts into a wholly free single Germany seems to me to be the natural destiny of the German people,

---

*(*Trans.*) Pierre Paul Royer-Collard (1763–1845). Politician and orator, leader of *doctrinaires* during the restoration of the monarchy.

**(*Trans.*) A high-profile French eco-demo issue (UK equivalent e.g. Sizewell B).

provided it accepts its present frontiers to the north, south, east and west, and is willing one day to join in a contractual organization of the whole of Europe for co-operation, freedom and peace' (press conference, 25 March 1959). It has taken about the same time for the nature of the Soviet Union's composition to come to light: its national and religious *sub-jecta* are resurfacing as predicted, and the Yalta expedient has exploded into the rest of Europe. 'Détente, entente and co-operation' – the Gaullian triptych, as it were – can take shape at last precisely because the blocs have disintegrated; notions like frontiers and territorial integrity (for example, the intangibility of the Oder–Neisse line, a leitmotiv of Gaullian diplomacy), which until recently were thought obsolete, are back on the agenda. Optimistic or maximalist exorcisms of these ideas – the Treaty of Rome, the Single European Act – are dwindling by the day. No pirouette, however exotic, can mask the fact that there can never be a federation anywhere without a federator. Or a security system that does not rest on a balance of hegemonies. Or a European structure that can neutralize or annul the balance of power between European nations. France was alone in the 1950s, under Mendès France, in rejecting the United States' conception of Europe as a European defence community. Later, in the 1960s, the Community partners demolished de Gaulle's alleged ambition to have a Europe under the tricolour. Now they may soon find themselves endorsing a Carolingian Europe, black and gold,* if Russia thinks it worth a try. What is certain is that – Community, Confederation or what have you – Europe in the year 2000 will not be in a state of weightlessness, a harmonious technostructure hovering above the national rivalries. While the ever-risky 'European concert' may be disguised or transcended, it can hardly be expected to disappear from human sight. But in terms of security for the immediate future, and without going into technical details, the old Gaullian picture of a continental Europe stretching from Brest to Brest-Litovsk, with or without the existing alliances (those more or less useful

---

*(*Trans.*) Colours of the German flag.

fakes), seems on the whole more plausible than the old socialist picture of an Atlantic Europe centred on NATO.

Neutralization of the New Germany? Disarmament?

As for making Germany a neutralized territory, this 'withdrawal' or 'disengagement' says nothing, in itself, of much value to us. For if this disarmament did not cover a zone that went as close to the Urals as to the Atlantic, what cover would France have? What then, in the event of conflict, would prevent a potential aggressor from crossing the undefended Germanic rampart in a single jump or short flight? What a narrow strip would then remain, between the Meuse and the Atlantic, for deployment of the West Europeans' resources! We are certainly in favour of the control and limitation of all weapons of war. But if these apparently humanitarian arrangements are not to risk leading to our disappearance, they must be applied to a zone deep enough and wide enough for France to be covered by them; and absolutely not, on the contrary, exposed.

I have not noticed a denser analysis of European disarmament in 1990. This one is signed by de Gaulle and dates from 1959. In 1950, the same old fossil wondered: 'Why should not the Rhine one day be a street in which Europeans will meet one another, instead of a ditch on whose banks they are perpetually fighting?' And in 1962 he was saying to the officers at Hamburg staff college: 'Organic co-operation between our armies with a view to arriving at a single, common defence set-up is essential for the union of our two countries.' An idea to which Chancellor Schmidt added volume and content in 1984.

But he also said:

There are those who cry: 'But what about Europe, a supranational Europe! It only needs putting together: the French with the Germans, the Italians with the English, and so on.' Well, you know, it's convenient and sometimes very tempting to chase after these chimeras and myths, but realities deal with one another on their own terms.

Of course nobody would dream of scrapping the Community's achievements, economic or political, which are also realities. The Europe of Brussels is a factor of prosperity and a reassuring political setting for all Europeans: it is not in any state's interests to renounce it. Who does not prefer to have several strings to his bow? But it would be utterly senseless for a great European country to put all the eggs of its future progress in the single basket of European unity. For two reasons: the first mistake would be to confuse *union*, which is necessary, with *unity*, which is impossible in a living mosaic whose historical dynamism has always been fuelled by differences and competition. Europe has lived by and through its national contrasts, and to eliminate them would be to annihilate it. A unified Europe is a non-Europe, something like a square circle. The second mistake would be to believe that peoples function according to some utilitarian principle, and are driven solely by the quest for commodities. After Freud, it ought to be recognized that the idea that 'people want what is good for them' is not entirely realistic.

Europe's present circumstances have revived the old-fashioned common-sense European, who does not believe that preparing the continent for Esperanto or 'integrated Volapük' is in its best interests. But the 'Gaullian' vision of world history owes its futurist quality to the paradoxes of the future itself. This is a matter not of strategy, but of the philosophy that governs it.

The sons of Condorcet and the apostles of MIT, French-style progressiveness and American-type modernism, are alike in their credulity. Both are very ill-equipped to understand the invariably retrograde character of progress. Believing with Ernest Labrousse that 'the social comes after the economic, and the mental comes after the social', they expect a sequence of logical connections to result in the social 'catching up' with the economic, then the mental with the social. But the paradox is that the intrusion of the new reactivates the old, modernity gives new life to archaism, and every scientific or technical revolution in the history of humanity has been balanced by secondary 'counter-revolutions' in people's attitudes and behaviour. That is why what Condorcet called 'barbarity' has never been eliminated. To give an example: you cannot open a McDonald's in Red Square without letting the priests back into St Basil's. The Shah of Iran a few years ago, like Gorbachev today, failed to register that the brutal destabilization of a society's ecosystem causes a convulsive reinforcement of the ancient stabilities under attack. In Iran, petroleum and motorways produced a massive backlash called 'the ayatollahs'. In the disunited Soviet Union, the equivalent recoil will be called by other names, equally obsolete and unknown to Marxists and liberals alike. The accelerated urbanization of the peasants in the Muslim–Arab world had the by-product of integralism: the simplest means for the uprooted populations of the new suburbs to get back to the country. In advanced Europe, new supranational powers have unleashed a regionalist revival, ranging from folklore to separatism, bagpipes* to bombs; the high-tech nomadism of objects and individuals turns models and dreams back towards their archaic roots. We could call this the 'jogging effect': the compulsion to run that afflicts metropolitan motorists who have given up walking. An ascending/descending spiral in which the previous stage can (of course) never be fully regained. In becoming more European we will become *more* German, Spanish or French, but not German, Spanish or French *in the same way* as before.

An acceleration of history, like the one we are living through at present, is not just a very quick passage from yesterday to tomorrow; it is also the abrupt reappearance in the present of the day before yesterday.

That is how 'the day before yesterday's man' can turn out to be the man of the day after tomorrow, which starts today; how a squire from old France can bridge the gap between the nineteenth and twenty-first centuries.

A vision of history that confuses man's relations with things and space with man's relations with man and time is one that confuses two radically different orders of reality. It amalgamates the cumulative and open history of science and technology, that of Jules Verne, with the repetitive and closed history of politics, that of Julius Caesar. Unable to count up to two, the brilliant minds of

---

*(*Trans.*) *Biniou*, the Breton variant of the notorious instrument.

economic and technical modernity are getting the future wrong with as sure a touch as their Saint-Simonian ancestors – bankers and polytechnicians just like them – who in 1860 were convinced that the spread of railways and the completion of the Suez Canal would bring the era of national wars and religious fanaticisms to a close.

It is because the twentieth century will have plumbed the depths of materialism that 'the twenty-first will be spiritual or will not take place'. Servan-Schreiber was a child, Malraux an adult.

All this suggests the conclusion that if you want to be innovative, you have to be (a little bit) old-fashioned. Like de Gaulle, who was entirely worthy of Jules Verne because he kept company with Julius Caesar. Virtuous Europeans accuse him of sowing a national wind in Europe and leaving us to reap the nationalist whirlwind. They fail to understand that whirlwinds can be largely prevented, by reaping the wind in good time.

10

Just run through that

for us again, would you?

No, absolutely not. Forget it. I may look the part, but I cannot bring myself to play the 'left-wing Gaullist'. Not, I hasten to add, through any concern for my personal image. Of all the rather silly subspecies in our botany, the Left-Gaullist is the frailest and least respected. I am only too well aware that our decision-makers check the weight before buying. No career has ever been built on uneasy awareness, and the left-wing Gaullist was ever the uneasiest of men. I find this disreputable image appealing and would assume it with pride, if it were not ruled out by my roots and the Hope principle.

There is what I am and there is what I believe.

To start with biography: I belong to the 'republican tradition'. That is my family. I vote with my own, come hell or high water. My country right or wrong. The long hexagonal past allotted me my place before I was born. Some days are more fun than others, but that is to be expected in 'the struggle of like against like' (as the Left opposition candidate so appositely called it in 1981). Although I have no special penchant for electoral geography, I know that the Order and the Mountain in 1849, the monarchists and republicans between 1857 and 1885, the Right and the Left in 1936, the Marshal and the terrorists in 1942, occupied pretty much the same bits of the map as the 'nationals' and democrats in 1965 and 1968. Class struggle is not – or is no longer – the motor of history, but the opposition between small and big, strong and weak, is no mere sociological flimflam. It is our spiritual and mental line of demarcation. Our great man – unfortunately for him, unfortunately for us – was on the wrong side, shoulder to shoulder with bishops, bosses and bigwigs. What we call 'winners'. He couldn't help it. He may well have wanted something different; he dreamed of going home on the metro every evening at six, he loathed his electorate in his heart of hearts; but it was his electorate, case closed. It is always a mistake for left-wingers (a deliciously 'retro' species, now that our leaders have embraced the winners' France) to rally to the smiling champions of the strong and big when they are looking friendly; for in a democracy a leader sooner or later has to line up with his troops, like a newspaper editor with his readers. However lucid the President may be, however open-minded the editor. I do not shop at *Le Figaro*, and I am not going to change now. Full stop.

Next, morality. I believe it is essential to clothe forces in forms, to repress the murderous collective libido by means of a no less collective *superego*: juridical, institutional, legislative. De Gaulle (perhaps I am mistaken) was a little quick to choose sides in the relations of force in the arena. To accept the intrinsic barbarity of international relations. To favour the deed over the statute. He did not take seriously such devices as the United Nations, the European Court of Justice, Amnesty International, the Human Rights Commission in Geneva, and all those improbable but unbreakable Committees for disarmament and so forth. They seemed, in fact, to enable the strong to play to the gallery while rendering the weak even weaker. True enough, but the machineries of sound law and good conscience do have other uses. I do not share the abstract piety with which the humanist Left regards Pacts, Conventions and Constitutions. This somewhat silly religion confuses forms with forces, as if history were made in council chambers, by commissions of sages. The Legalist Left – that of Briand, Blum, Mitterrand – knows nothing of tempests, currents, tides and winds. It mistakes the canal for the ocean. But I still share this impossible wish: to subject nature to contract, bring law to the forests, and make history civilized. One has to recognize that the nature of things is inhuman, and do everything possible to humanize it. One has to anticipate a bit of Hitler and Stalin in our Europe of tomorrow, for war is the untranscendable horizon of all societies, archaic, industrial or postmodern. Yet another reason for clearing blue patches in the unending grey storm, for bringing moments of justice into the eternal massacre. Is nature the only thing that 'works'? Yes, but *Homo sapiens* is the only animal that does not go along with nature. I have no intention of leaving. I remain with those who seek the squaring of the circle.

Old Man de Gaulle, like a scientist, had clearly identified the forces at work in the worldwide dynamic of peoples. He was good at manipulation, and hardly ever made a wrong decision. There is nothing more to say about all that. It keeps the water out. It is 'operational'. I could be a Gaullist if I had to, but only physically, not politically or metaphysically.

Because all the same, operations of that sort are hardly ideal.

So the Left is stuck with the impossible. Our utopia is to make history; our excuse, that we are subject to it; our task, to inflect it.

*

Now the ideal is lying abandoned in the nettles. We no longer inflect the course of things: law of the highest bidder inside, law of the strongest outside. We hardly dare look at ourselves in the mirror and think about our impotence. What François Mitterrand called *The Socialism of the Possible* in 1971 has become, twenty years later, actual liberalism tempered with hopeful rhetoric. The grand coalition of those who, after '68, said *no* to the *nature of things* has subsided twenty years later into a more or less evasive and sheepish *yes* to the *force of things*. What would have been thought of a president of the radical Council under the Third Republic if he had allowed the Church to repossess secular education? The same thing that would have been thought of a Socialist president under the Fifth who, after two seven-year terms, allowed TV – our own public education medium – to be swallowed up by the advertising industry.

In this context, digging up the man of 18 June is a way of reviving the left-winger inside us. Of making him return to the moral and intellectual sources of the *no*. To our secret mainspring, our *raison d'être*.

The message is simple and still subversive: whoever you are, Europe or nation, tendency or party, man or woman, resist. Be yourself, do not lose heart under the weight of catcalls and opinion polls, do not dress up the adoption of compromise as the system of government by calling it 'government culture'.

Not too sure about that any more? Well then, be *really* cynical and remember the law: whoever wants to win has to begin by losing. Wanting to be in on everything straight away is the surest way of being in on nothing.

A little Gaullism takes one away from the values of republican democracy; a lot brings one back to them. At the end of this detour through what people will call the Right, here I am back in my natural place: the Left of the Republic.

Meaning?

Meaning we should note the end of a cycle, a low ebb of the European and French Left, and get ready now for the next high tide: *corso* and *ricorso*, as Vico would call them.

*

The end of a secular cycle, in the slow tempo of gradual change.*
Let us make the point succinctly.

The past hundred years have sapped the sociological, medio-logical and ideological foundations of the socialist movement in the industrial West. The Second International, which celebrated its centenary in 1989 along with the automobile, is still moving from the shove provided by the first Industrial Revolution. But along the way our klaxon-horned roadster has lost its fuel tank, its engine and its headlights.

Its *tank* or *source* of social energy fell off when the socialist Left could no longer define itself as the spokesman of the 'working classes', the champion of the exploited against the exploiters. Now that production is no longer dominated by material labour and information is supplanting energy, the factory has stopped being the centre of society and working time the centre of life. When society is no longer divided into two opposing groups of classes united by common interest, but increasingly into cultural (national, religious, linguistic) and natural (age or sex) groups, then there is no 'chosen class'; but a steady growth of corporatisms

---

*(*Trans.*) *Dans le temps long,* a historian's technical term for the rhythm of gradual mutation through trends.

that set white-collar workers – around four-fifths of the population – against each other.

It lost its engine or *medium* when the party form had been emptied like a whelk-shell by television, the breakdown of family life and the decline of the written word. The rival leaders flash their blades on the small screen for anyone who is interested, but their eyes are on the pundit or presenter, not the list of militant motions. After the death of the party as 'alternative society' (with newspapers, choral groups, crèches and correct values), then of the party as 'pilot of change', we are currently witnessing the death throes of the party as a setting for collective effort and thought, made redundant by the new means of communication. This decline parallels that of Parliament as the centre of gravity for civic deliberation.

Finally, the Left has lost its missionary *bearings*. Messianism about progress and the Manichaeism of the class struggle, those by-products of bygone systems of oppression, having – not before time – vanished from its agenda, it is disorientated, no longer privy to the secrets of Providence. Having learned that a political programme has no effect on exchange rates or inflation differentials, it has become so suspicious of social plans and expectations that it sees the slightest intellectual effort as something suspect, damaging to its credibility, liable to make it look like an irresponsible, nostalgic dreamer.

The result is a breakdown in the driver's imagination and a lot of bickering in the back seat. Locked in their petty quarrels, the socialists have lost sight of the big picture.

It is good that socialism, which used to be a Church, a scholastics and a religious faith, should mature into a lay and secular adulthood, even at the cost of some militant energy. It would be fatal for its will to remain broken down for long. The Right, which defends material interests, can afford pragmatism; the Left is condemned to long-term vision. But when it comes to winning the next election or reducing the budgetary deficit, just watch it hiding in economic realism like an ostrich in the sand. Comfortable in designer armchairs, dispatching current affairs with a practised hand, it is surrendering its soul.

In Communism there was a hideous mystification and a

grandiose myth. Lenin dead? The social democrats said so when he was still alive, when the Communists split with the workers' movement. Marx in a coma? The Scandinavians took their leave of the Big Beard in the 1920s, the Germans at Bad Godesberg in 1959, the Spanish in 1979, the French in 1982. Not only were the sins of Communism none of their doing, but they analysed them better than anyone else. But now that they are left with sole responsibility for carrying the emancipation project forward, it is clear that they have given it up themselves. Rather an irksome development: Hamlet has put on the crown, but is now wondering why he exists. Disillusioned by management, made colourless by the obsession with majorities, rendered stale by mediatized demagogy, the victorious and disenchanted Western socialists have nothing left to offer the orphans of utopia. Except – the product of a double setback that should have made them stronger, the failure of liberalism to redistribute and Communism to produce – 'the alliance of an open economy with social justice'. Economic capitalism to produce wealth; political socialism to redistribute it via an umpire state. This sober recipe does not arouse quite the same enthusiasm as the mystique of the great upheaval. Just as well. But it will still need to correspond in some way with observable behaviour. For in reality, whatever may be said to mask its absence from strategy and its unending postponement through successive 'phases', social justice comes *behind* economic efficiency. In people's minds as in life, the bottom is on top, and vice versa. 'What are we for? – To implement the Right's policies, but in acceptable form.' Having given up competing for power with the powerful, the Left at best sets itself up as a counter-power, a discreet factor of balance. It is no longer a source of historic projects, but an apparatus for curbing a universal mercantilist movement which it clearly believes to be irresistible. When it fights it does so defensively, in rearguard style. Normally it goes along with the movement: that is where it 'succeeds'. *Eppur se muove*, you may say. Yes, but used incorrectly or as a substitute for something else. As if socialism were good for anything, except socialism. Felipe González modernized Spain by opening it to international capitalism. Willy Brandt gave great service to the cause of German unity. Mitterrand democratized the Fifth Republic by legitimizing alternation. The Italian Communist Party – the Italian expression of social democracy – will continue to promote Italian integration into the European space, as it did in opposition. All of them have given unstinting help to economic modernization, to the principle of nationality, to democracy, to Europe ... to everything except 'the workers' cause', their historical identity card. Do I need to point out that deregulating capital movements in the liberal Europe of 1992, reducing taxes on capital earnings, turning the screw on wage taxation and impoverishing the redistributing state, will hardly help European socialists to achieve their declared aim of modernizing and democratizing society?

There are periods of history in which the progressive has negative responsibilities. It is already established that there is no alternative to the worldwide *dynamic* of the market. Social democrats will be doing a great service for humanity if they can suggest some alternative to the worldwide *dictatorship* of the market. If only by protecting a few oases of inventiveness and worth – culture, public education, the environment, television, scientific research – from mercantile relations of production. But to launch and maintain a counter-dynamic of this sort, to block the advent of the planetary supermarket (given the vast cost in energy of the work of social transformation, which leaves the individual grizzled militant with a feeling of dilapidation and disarray), we would have to keep intact an inner, personal rejection of the system's poisons and delights. Instead of rolling in them like pigs in shit, and promising to turn over a new leaf tomorrow.

'I don't want a post. I want a job of work.' So said Colonel Rossel when he offered his services to the Paris Commune after Sedan.* He was sick of 'generals guilty of surrender' and believed that 'resistance always has a good chance'. (This direct antecedent of the temporary brigadier-general of 1940 was right in the long term but unluckier than his successor: he was shot soon afterwards by the reactionary Versailles troops, who had surrendered to the Prussians, and who emerged victorious.)

---

*(*Trans.*) Rossel, the only professional soldier to join the Paris Commune in 1871, became its Defence Minister.

Socialism has secured all the posts and lost its job of work. A very commonplace sort of mishap: the world is populated by soulless bodies, more often than not. Our national Left has been tamed from top to bottom, inserted in the client chain, granted its share of celebrity. It is a being whose *raison d'être* fell unnoticed by the wayside as it allowed itself, little by little, to succumb to the sweets of power. It is all extremely banal.

There is not much chance that militants who have invested their lives in 'the construction of a free and just society' will get a return on their investment. They have made a loss. Our society is free, sort of; but it is not very just – indeed, rather less so than ten years ago, if the statistics are right. I understand and sometimes share their feelings. They wonder what alternation is good for. Anyone can see who it is good for, but the whole business – posts, government, France, Europe: for what? So that ministers can talk about themselves, live on a grand scale, frequent other powerful men, those jack o-lanterns of relentless time? Is it just a matter of getting an *ism* to their names and seeing their mugs on the telly? We wanted to change programmes, to switch channels. To move from private to public, for example. The change that occurred was in the other direction. From the competitive pursuit of maximum profit to co-operation between individuals for a common purpose: here, too, the wrong direction. We had had enough of hearing people talk about the heart as if it were the nose, and here at last were the equations for happiness: Modern socialism = minimum wage + audience ratings; Justice = charity + cynicism. That is how it is in our high society, where the technocrat rubs shoulders with stars of stage and screen. I understand your disappointment, my friends. But such is the law of (human) nature, and anyway there is progress, of a sort, in disillusion. In the year 1000, people expected Christ and got Rome. In 1917 they expected the Proletariat and got the Bureaucracy and the Police. In 1981 they expected socialist self-management, and got sound administration of the ambient capitalism, for Europe's sake. It must be admitted, though, that Bérégovoy in place of Jaurès was a lot less disastrous than Beria instead of Soviets. We should not complain too bitterly. Nor should we be shocked if changes that abolish the differences between currencies, standards of living and productivity norms also make liberal-minded socialists interchangeable with social-minded liberals. And we should not make socialist leaders shoulder all the blame for the duplicity of our whole society, divided as it is between the cult of modernity and a nostalgic dream of justice. It is no easy thing to defend advantages already secured while continuing to promote equality, to combine today's things with yesterday's words. The schizophrenia of the socialist in power belongs primarily to his constituents. The most that can be required of him is that he devote as much attention to the transparency of his own management as to that of the Stock Exchange.

In other respects our socialist leaders will soon be irreproachable. It might have been feared that with neophyte enthusiasm they would end up by becoming more African than Foccart, more Atlanticist than Washington, more protective of the franc than Raymond Barre, more corrupt than the average party, sharper than the ordinary international financier, more feathered and sequined than the norm for the show-biz state: in a word, more establishment than the establishment. But age and experience have helped them to find a relaxed cruising speed. So that in everything – broadcasting and the public sector, observance of the new European disciplines, incomes policy, taxation, alignment with the practices of our neighbours – our realists can be seen extending the probability curves with sober firmness, like any other experienced manager optimizing the performance of a working company. Instead of intruding 'irrational' or 'dysfunctional' elements by indulging in irresponsible criticism.

Will the function of the socialist Left in Europe turn out to have been the invention of capitalism with a human face? This was not on the programme of the founding fathers but, as everyone knows, programmes are there to be bypassed and forgotten. It would mean that socialism would die the victim of its own practical success in modifying primitive capitalism's *modus operandi* from the outside. If that is what it was for, then its mission is accomplished and it can retire to its texts and its meetings.

There remains a somewhat risky alternative: abandoning our scruples and rejoining a world which will soon be brought face to face with itself, without excuses or distractions, by the disappearance of its internal and external enemies. There are worse things than a trashed biosphere, decayed cities, an imploding Third World, stock market crashes and monetary crisis (all more or less curable maladies, perhaps resulting from progress). There is the void gouged under a way of life rendered increasingly meaningless by the absurd short-term logic of profit for the sake of profit and production for the sake of production. We may soon have to learn that the great ideologies whose collapse we celebrated with such competitive verve were less bloody, in the final analysis, than the tribal and confessional fanaticisms that are due to replace them (for like nature itself, human nature abhors a vacuum).

For two centuries the West, with the colonized world on its heels, has been passing from revolt to revolution. From emotional and regressive violence – *Jacquerie* or riot – to reasoned, universalist violence directed towards a valid future for all mankind, as the French, Russian and Chinese revolutions imagined it. The foundering of regimes claiming to offer universal hope has raised the possibility, in the northern hemisphere as well as the southern, of a return journey from World Revolution to tribal revolt. Will scorched earth and fire in the blood make us regret the passing of Reason's totalitarianisms?

It may fall to what remains of the Left to reinvent socialism as method (in place of yesterday's utopia), if ethnic and religious cannibalism is to be prevented from destroying civilized humanity. It might then be possible to bypass the historical sterility of revolts, and move on from false revolution to real reform. It would be worth trying, even if there were only the slimmest chance of success.

But it will not happen unless people are first willing to risk defying the law of the milieu, their own milieu. To preserve their critical faculty and their political judgement, as well as their personal free will. As de Gaulle once did, in the face of his own social milieu and the Europe of his time.

*

François Mitterrand has done great service to the well-meaning Left by subjecting it to the ordeal of reality. It was only to be expected that in trampling on its dreams and repressing its anger, he would also break its mainspring.

If you think too much about the future, you desert the present, leaving the adversary a clear field. This is the purist temptation, that of the tub-thumping Left. If you pay too much attention to the present, you desert the future. This could be the temptation of the managerial Left: capitulation by infinitesimal stages. Sectarianism, opportunism ... every defect has its time in a sort of biological pulse, a vital ebb and flow.

And the flow should be turning back towards the time of principles, for the time of expedient arrangements is drawing to a close.

*

As a rough rule of thumb, a party only functions properly for about twenty years: it may survive longer, but beyond that period it has outlived its usefulness. A regime, a team or an individual in power can carry out its work of transformation for only about ten years; it may last longer, of course, but after that period it begins to rattle and shake.

Afterwards, *dura lex sed lex*, you clear everything away and start again. You can make a new start only by making a clean sweep, conserve by destroying: metamorphosis, transformation, reincarnation. Law of nature.

François Mitterrand has taught us to dedramatize the events of history, to model them on 'everyday things'. He would be the first to discourage us from dramatizing the end of the generation, of the Mitterrand dream. A passage from *corso* to *ricorso*, from one coil of the spiral to another.

Who is going to intercept the ball, to launch the return match and score the first point?

It will have to be someone capable of making bridges between de Gaulle and us, between yesterday and tomorrow. Someone able to adapt for action a few very simple rules of conduct, indispensable to any political purpose. While ridding us of the three millstones that hold us back: the libertarian illusion, the contemporary illusion and the economic illusion.

Is the best way to avoid renouncing your ideas to give up having them altogether? Not really. It is better to renovate them by adapting to the paradoxical permutation of old and new as one period succeeds another.

*

For the past twenty years or so, the more or less openly admitted ideal of the Left avant-garde has been promotion of the *zero institution*. We will not argue here about whether this fallacy on the conditions for exercising liberty dates from ''68' or not; or whether it owes a theoretical debt to Michel Foucault (who blazed so many false trails). To set the individual above the institution is a mirror-image response to the authoritarian Right's placing of the institution before the individual, and every bit as harmful: both have the same result, robbing the subject of freedom of judgement and action. This applies on all levels: child and family, pupil and school, soldier and army, deputy and Parliament, average man and legal system, citizen and Republic. In no instance does it serve the individual's cause to humble the institution. For it is the symbolic that creates the social bond, not the other way round. Man is an institutional being, *dependent on mediations,* and the search for *maximum immediacy* in every area undermines the foundations of his freedom. A consumer may not need founders or institutions; but a citizen does. When the symbolic is dissolved by the spontaneous, or rules by feelings (as love may be dissolved by desire), the result is usually the death of what was supposed to be liberated: desire, vitality, inventiveness.

This general movement has been validated among us by the view that there should be 'less State'. It ignores the fact that the individual's autonomy in relation to the state is meaningful only if the state keeps its own autonomy in relation to society. And the fact that nobody is free in a nation that has stopped being free. The first millennium in Europe saw the elimination of what remained of public power, the last guarantee of free status for the lower classes; primary feudalization led to the return of 'private' powers and the enslavement of the peasantry. Will the year 2000 see a second feudalization of Europe (second serfdom, so to speak)? It seems probable. The new lords – lords of money now, not land, like Italian *condottieri* – have got their paws on the means of communication, of production, of exchange. Clerical powers are vying for the remains of public education; ethnic and confessional communities are trying to carve their own allotments from the remnants of the public domain. To struggle against the auctioning of public property is to resist the enslavement and banalization of the individual. A century from now, perhaps, the new serfs of businesses, fiefs, regions and Churches will look back on the Capetian de Gaulle as a pioneer of the new resistance to the new Middle Ages.

This struggle requires an instrument: the state. 'It is not there to give pleasure, but to generate effort. Failing that, it would lose its purpose and disappear,' de Gaulle wrote in a letter a year before his death. The language of energy – all those quaint calls for effort, ardour, self-denial – has an antediluvian ring in our asthenic, demotivated society, so cleverly justified by trendy sociologists, whose stock in trade is making a virtue of necessity. In terms of the individual and collective psyche, communication observes the 'pleasure principle': that is why its internal constraints suit the inner drives of individualist societies, in which humour and love are collective values. The TV-state is a state for eliminating effort, a disappearing state. The ethic of the Fourth Republic is making a vigorous comeback at present, because at last the technology exists to realize its ambition: to avoid distressing anyone. But the fact is that when a country cannot be first economically, it has all the more reason to stay in front politically (without, of course, giving up the economic struggle). You can quibble about the need for socialism in tomorrow's European societies, but there is no doubt at all that France in Europe, even more than its neighbours, will need a state. And statesmen. It will not take long to understand what the *pleasure-state* could cost all of us. With its incoherence and impulsiveness, its alternation of whims and absences, its enslavement to the rhythm of 'interventions', 'local interests', popularity polls and electoral terms; with its penury of clear ideas and long-term views. Which is going to be more damaging to liberty in the long run: a strong state, or a sovereign civil society? Today's prejudices are a pretty poor training for the paradoxes of tomorrow.

Another mirage is the opposition between the contemporary

and the archaic that underlies our cult of the present. 'Since –
despite itself – 1968 liberated us from utopia, meaning the past,
while 1981 emancipated us from doctrine, meaning the future, we
can now try to live in the present,' Jacques Julliard once wrote. In
a word: freedom is ours, and real life can begin. It was an attractive
idea, but sadly unfounded. We are supposed to think our society
adult because it no longer feeds on words, without noticing its
infantile gorging on images. Living exclusively in the present is the
surest way to enter the future looking in the wrong direction. That
is why yesterday's trendies are left hanging in midair while de
Gaulle, the archetypal non-trendy, survives changes of climate
relatively well.

Everything conspires to set a high value on ephemera: the
dictatorship of information that becomes valueless overnight
('Who wants yesterday's papers?' – the Rolling Stones); the
dictatorship of capitalism, maximum profit in minimum time; the
dictatorship of feeling, which varies from day to day and feeds off
itself. Without forgetting the timelessness of 'human rights', our
official ideology, ahistorical and, by the same token, audiovisual
('Should Louis XVI have been condemned to death? No, of course
not, how ghastly!'). The moralizing depoliticization of youth
fostered by governmental socialism sacrifices the right of peoples
to self-determination to Human Rights writ large: a mirror-image
of the inverse sacrifice promoted by Stalinism and the Third-
Worldisms of recent years. Here at home, human rights are a staple
of the chronicles; everywhere else, the right of peoples is turning
the chronology upside down. Surely it is possible to keep them
both in mind, as de Gaulle did in his day?

It is always pleasant to get out of a history which is so consistently
immoral and distasteful. But our pleasures are not always available
to order, and we can find ourselves forced back in.

'I've been saying it for a thousand years,' de Gaulle is alleged to
have growled at a sceptic who bothered him with queries about
Franco–German reconciliation. Futurist humour. Seeing through
short-term illusion to the history behind the event seems to be the
most urgent need. Usually people try to unbolt the ephemeral
with long-term forecasts, as if the depth of time did not accumulate
in both directions, backwards as well as forwards, the one because

of the other. The man who went to French Canada in 1967 to pay a debt incurred by Louis XV was widely mocked. It did not occur to anyone that this formidable capacity for *recall* might be balanced by an equal faculty for *anticipation*. Bergson likened the effectiveness of the man of action to the working of a bow and arrow: 'the further back his representation is stretched, the greater the force with which he flies forward'. Memory may well be even more revolutionary tomorrow than it was yesterday (when I allowed myself to coin the saying). Not just because amnesiacs bring about their own oblivion, nor because men without memories are men without projects. But because the way actuality flattens out our representations of the world daily reinforces the unjust status quo. Has the scrapping of the entire theoretical and historical memory of French socialism by our young management cadres produced a renewal, or a disintegration? To each his own object lessons.

The technocrats who are fabricating European institutions without reference to European history, cobbling things together on paper for the future – 'a real executive at the top of the Community', 'a development agency' – will discover not only that these artefacts are insubstantial, but that manipulating economic and juridical spaces, without taking their corresponding depth of time into account, makes things go backwards.

The other decoy of our time is the Economy and Finance superstition. Some will say that this is a much-needed compensation for decades of economic impracticality. But pointing out to our decision-makers that there are levels of reality, important ones, that have nothing to do with goods and services is not a call for a return to the wishful thinking of earlier recovery programmes. Pointing out that the victory of the long over the short term, the profound over the superficial, always gives a country's culture revenge on its technostructure, does not imply that people should forget about the daily rates of the franc. On this point the public mind is in danger of being lulled by the social prestige of our big managers. Waking it up would be a job for a socialist who was more interested in the realities than in his own image. In the long term it is always worthwhile to stay in touch with the depths, where there are no monetary instruments or signs, but images and a spirit. 'Traditionalism is the megalomania of misery,' a Central European

dissident once observed. A cheeky Westerner might add that economism is the idiocy of abundance. The bottomless contempt of most French intellectuals for Francophone culture, echoed by the courteous indifference of our governments, gives some idea of what our Finance Inspectors think the word 'culture' means: spectacular pageantry first, *haute couture* second, fine arts a poor third. The agreeably superfluous; budgetary surplus devoted to the management of vanities: decorations, 'Césars' and 'Sept d'or'.*
If we let these necessary side-issues blind us to the real stakes of civilization, we will be swimming against the tide of Europe's long history. Remember that Romanian 'totalitarianism', apparently hewn from granite, fell to pieces just because a little Transylvanian priest insisted on saying Mass in Hungarian. A culture is enormously *heavy*, compared to a party leadership or a rate of profit. A language, a religion, a memory, are immaterial granite: mess with them at your peril. Could it be that we in the West, for all our self-assurance and snobberies, are rather *lightweight* in our perception of these active subterranean masses?

Communism, as a political force and cultural project, was overturned by its own economic incapacity. The world of free enterprise has achieved, by comparison, tremendous economic success and a very acceptable political compromise. But there is still a grave cultural threat, because uncontrolled and unlimited economic growth may cause the long-term cultural and ecological devastation of the planet. We have yet to see the bottom line of the liberal model's balance sheet.

In any case, democratic capitalism will be deluding itself if it imagines that the master of the battlefield *controls* it, and that history has come to a halt with its triumph. Its undeniable present victory carries the seeds of a possible long-term defeat, once the *economic illusion* it shared with its late challenger has been dissipated. Liberalism and Marxism concurred for a century on the same presupposition: that in the hierarchy of serious matters economics came first, before politics, with culture (a matter for

---

· *(Trans.)* Show-business awards, like Oscars and Emmies.

ladies and mincing impresarios) coming last. The day is not far off when it will be realized that their real order of precedence is the other way round: that culture comes before politics, which is more important than economics. The first thing human groups want in our post-industrial world is to be themselves: to speak their own language, practise their own beliefs, nourish their own creativity in a preserved living environment. Next, they want to be able to take part in public life as citizens responsible for themselves. And lastly, they want to produce a sufficiency and distribute it equitably.

The future belongs to someone from the Left who, with or without the aid of some special charisma, manages to persuade colleagues and others that human beings become inventive, get off the ground, only when they can define themselves as beings of institution, memory and freedom. Something of the sort, surely, is what drove an obscure Secretary of State for War across the Channel to London that day in June 1940. Needless to say, personal resentments were rumoured: he would never have left if Pétain had made him a minister.... What do you expect, murmured the Marshal with a shrug, of a disappointed officer, 'ungrateful, haughty and embittered'.

Strange how quick people are to believe allegations of baseness, and how slow to admit other possibilities.

*

In 1986 or thereabouts, the monthly *Globe* discerned on the horizon 'all the early signs of a soft society'. 'It is time to have done with romantic visions.' We should not be too surprised when the *hard* comes charging in, with its own Romanticism for better or for worse. 'Passion in politics? Had it up to here, nearly died of it,' our myopic lookouts say. They are right in a way. But in avoiding Charybdis our friends will ram Scylla; for apathy leads, with absolute inevitability, to the triumph of Romanticism – for worse.

He is deeply naive, the orphan of dead beliefs who seeks salvation in disenchanted indifference, by reinventing the timeless, defeated figure of the credulous sceptic. You do not stop the cohorts of Allah or Pétain with elegant unbelief; that takes 'militants' of a *different sort*: believers without fanaticism.

Everywhere – in architecture, painting, cinema – anaesthesia by eclecticism, by frivolity dressed up as 'postmodernism', is coming to an end. The threads are slack: 'time to retighten', as Paul Virilio says. To find the key string, and pull. Everywhere.

Which means first recognizing the primacy of the end over the means; of the idea over the individuals who put it into effect. That alone can nourish a strategy, an aesthetic, a morality of tension. And on the heels of fervour, effective action. Political activity is fast becoming a matter not of solving problems but of exploiting them to improve or rectify one's personal image. On both sides of the political divide, egoism has raised image-marketing to the level of collective delusion, producing an every-man-for-himself, crabs-in-a-barrel situation. The manipulative indifferentism which has become our habit slackens and disunites us. The question is whether the next century will be able to invent a form of spiritual intensity without dogmatic exclusivity. Fraternity without crony-dom. Time is short.

A united France, a united socialism, a united Europe? Of course, of course. Why not? But people unite around their aims. And these aims are attained in reality only if they are transcended in the imagination, which is why exemplary images and myths of identi-fication are needed. This is the function of the great man. Nietzsche was wrong to say that the great man is an end in himself, that sterility dogs his footsteps, that he can only reign over a benighted people. The true virtue of the great character is that he inspires others to appear, in an infectious ricocheting of ideals called a culture.

That man is small, whatever his rank or position, whose end is himself. Great, who accepts that there is something greater than himself and freely subordinates himself to it. Like St Ignatius to God, Jaurès to justice, the lover to the beloved, the sportsman to his sport. A researcher to his research, an artist to his talent, a rebel to his cause. And de Gaulle, artist, rebel and believer, to his France.

It may not be your France, or altogether mine. But in paying your respects to de Gaulle, you will also be saluting in advance those still unknown who, one day, will stalk our field of ashes and raise the living.